When I was five we lived in the house on the hill. It was a magical place: an old New England farmhouse surrounded by a nine acre wood and high grassy meadow overlooking the river and the town. On the river side, the land tumbled away down a cliff--a craggy granite ledge which a former owner had equipped with a Victorian iron railing and a crudely cut path and steps. I would imagine I was one of the ladies with a parasol in my grandmother's photographs as I tripped along the path in delicately heeled high-button shoes, carrying the train of my traveling costume. It was our favorite way to reach the road below and provided wonderful sites for hide-and-seek! Deep in the wood was a mica mine—treasure in the heart of darkness! Standing behind the house a row of tall pines— giant pines to a five-year-old—! a broad swing with ropes reached up into the sky...the smell of pine needles and the sense of height, the soaring whoosh! of pine boughs, and the dizzy motion of ecstatic swinging all come _____ me when I remember the ho_____ the hill. We lived there only ____ year while the church found _____ nage on a more sedate and _____ ious street. But for me, the _____ the hill with its atmosphere _____ to the past and to nature, _____ ation above the town and in _____ mind above the river will alw_____ the seat of childhood fantasy, filled with the sounds and color and scents of imagination, the dreams of darkness and adventure that continue to feed my soul as an adult. and an

This book (and other Soleil Press publications on the subject of
lifewriting, including books, manuals, workbook, and binders for
teachers and individuals interested in writing their personal and
family histories) is available at volume discount for bulk pur-
chases for promotions, premiums, fund-raising and educational
use. For details, please contact Soleil Press at the address below.

PRINTED IN U.S.A.
FIRST EDITION

SOLEIL ✳ PRESS
95 GOULD ROAD, #14 LISBON FALLS, MAINE 04252
207-353-5454 ✳ memoirs@i me.net
Visit our website: http: / / www.Turningmemories. com
Represented in Australia by
Rae Luckie Associates, 15 Belvedere Street, Kiama,
NSW 2533. Telephone: 0242-323-988

PUBLISHERS CATALOGUING IN PUBLICATION DATA
Ledoux, Denis
The Photo Scribe, A Writing Guide/How to Write the Stories
        Behind Your Photographs
1. Creative Writing.-2. Autobiography.-3. Crafts
I.Title
ISBN: 0–9619373–4–3
LC # 98-090625

BOOK DESIGN: Martha Blowen
AUTHOR PHOTO: J. Felice Boucher, Brunswick, Maine
INTERIOR PHOTOS: Thanks to Sally Lunt, Jill Grogg, Amy Grogg,
Emily Brown, Posey Lippincott, Ledoux and Blowen families.
SPECIAL THANKS to Steve Samson and Lynda Arsenault at First
Choice Printing.

The Photo Scribe

A Writing Guide

How to Write the Stories Behind Your Photographs

by Denis Ledoux

Acknowledgements

Without Sally Lunt, Soleil Press office manager, no project of this scope could be undertaken. We are grateful for her many talents, not the least of which are her optimism and efficiency. In our best moments, we are optimists, too. This trait is confirmed by the wondrous serendipity by which both Sally and our new assistant, Jill Grogg, who arrived in time to work on this book, have found us, each at a crucial time in our development. Thanks to them both for their valuable contributions to Soleil Press.

A number of Turning Memories Into Memoirs™ teachers and workshop leaders were kind enough to read and comment on advance copies of this manuscript. Their insight and generosity are much appreciated. They are Rae Luckie, of Kiama, New South Wales; Dianne Aoki, of Honolulu; Carole Cole, of Bountiful, Utah; Margaret DeAngelis, of Harrisburg, Pennsylvania; Jim O'Leary, of Albuquerque; and Audrienne Womack, of Washington, D.C.

We have been fortunate to have college interns work with us during the year of this book's preparation. These young people have jazzed up the office with their energy and enthusiasm and have been generous with their time and skills: Bates College writing interns Ethan Craig and Megan Albrecht, thank you very much. We also acknowledge a special debt to Peter Payette, whose presence and dedication this spring and summer were invaluable contributions to our efforts on this and many other projects. Thanks, Peter.

Bryce Muir, with characteristic generosity, was very helpful at the (we thought) eleventh hour: thank you!

Our special thanks will ever go to Ladora and Lucille, and to Maxim and Zoé, the generations who surround us with love and purpose and from whom we continue to learn every day.

—D. L., M. B.

Dedication

This book is for the scrapbookers I first met
at the Creative Memories Showcase 1996 in St. Cloud, MN
—women whose energy and enthusiasm for their work,
whose willingness to share their spirit freely,
and whose dedication to affirming and preserving
their personal and family histories
has continued to be an inspiration to me. . .

and for

scrapbookers and families everywhere
who are preserving stories
in their photo albums.

–D.L.

Also by Denis Ledoux

Turning Memories Into Memoirs
  A Handbook for Writing Lifestories

What Became of Them
  and Other Stories from Franco-America

Mountain Dance and Other Stories

Lives In Translation: An Anthology of
  Contemporary Franco-American Writings

Table of Contents

Preface

"My photos tell only a part of my family story. How can I include more of it in my albums?" scrapbook consultants asked in both 1996 and 1997 when I presented writing workshops at the national conventions of Creative Memories™ (CM). CM is an international company that promotes and teaches photosafe*[1] scrapbooking awareness through classes and workshops.

My album looks great. Now I want it to tell the story I remember when I look at it.

Since 1988, I have helped thousands of people to write their personal and family lifestories* through my Turning Memories Into Memoirs™ workshops. Because of my experience, CM invited me to teach their consultants what scrapbookers call *photojournaling*. I taught them how to write interesting and effective narrative texts—*cameo narratives,** I call them—to incorporate into the well-designed, photo-safe photograph albums they produce and advocate.

CM consultants were eager to add new skills to their album-making. They knew instinctively that

---

[1] Words marked with an asterisk are defined in the Glossary (p.117) as well as within the text.

learning to write more than a brief caption would satisfy their own needs to tell more complete stories and would enhance their work with customers who longed to create family-legacy albums.

An autobiography in my albums—I never thought of my photos that way before.

Consultants wanted to tell a complete lifestory (personal or family story)—but in their albums, not in book-length autobiographies* or biographies* people often produce in my Turning Memories™ workshops. They were not, and didn't want to be, writers first and album–makers second.

"My photo albums are where I want to record my lifestory," they said. "How can I integrate more text into them and still have the photos be central to the album?"

This book answers that question. In *The Photo Scribe*, you, too, will learn to tell your lifestory, or, if you choose, portions of it, using both photographs and short, well-written texts.

I call the family-legacy album that results from combining photos and text the "lifestory photo album."* And I call the process of creating it "photoscribing."*

Introduction

Photos are the driving force behind the story told in most albums—no photo, no story. It shouldn't be that way! In *The Photo Scribe,* you will learn to tell a lifestory using the events and relationships of your life, not the photos you happen to have on hand, as your primary organizing element. This principle, more than any other presented in *The Photo Scribe,* will help you to transform photos, captions,* and cameo narratives into meaningful lifestory photo albums.

I wish had a picture of that moment. I wish there were a way I could keep that memory alive.

Telling Your Lifestory

Photos depict an external version of our lives. They only capture material, visual things—leaving the viewer to guess about the deeper, sometimes hidden meaning.

The complexities of a given situation or experience may seem too difficult or embarrassing to put into words—so we leave them out and stick to names and dates. Or we let those parts of the story show up in the storyline we

I'll note you in my book of memory.
—Shakespeare

speak—perhaps in an off-hand manner—to a friend as we leaf through the pages of the album. This oral sharing fills the need we have for the more complex story to be communicated—but the spoken words exist only briefly. Once we have finished speaking, the story is again at risk of being forgotten.

Your Stories Are at Risk

Let's say you have begun to place your photos in albums and to give some thought to arranging them on a well-designed page. Let's say you have been careful to label each picture with an identifying caption such as: "Simpson's Beach, 1985."

Every time you look at that photo of your time at the beach, a flood of memories washes over you. You recall that it was that day, as you watched a couple playing with their toddler, that you decided you were ready to have a child and to quit your unsatisfying job. Your experience of making that life decision that day at the shore is still vivid to you as you look at the familiar image.

But the caption says only "Simpson's Beach, 1985." None of what was most significant about that time and place is recorded in your album. How can you, even if you want to, record a decision (or the feelings that went into it) in a photo? You can't! But, you *can* write a narrative* to put next to the photo.

> On this beach, I watched the couple next to us playing with their two-year-old. Their pleasure in being with him was so obvious that I realized I wanted more than anything to be a parent, too. It was more important than the stressful job at Nichols that I was

trying to hold on to. Nothing else seemed to matter after that.

You'll notice that this cameo narrative is quite different from (and reveals a lot more than) the sort of comment line that reads:

Sun 'n' Sand. What a beach day!

Without a thoughtful narrative, the story of what was important at Simpson's Beach is a secret in the process of being lost— even though a well-preserved photograph presents the sun, the water, and the smile on your face. With the narrative, though, the vacation photo takes its place as a more complex record of a special time in your life and a turning point in your family's history.

I've changed so much! An old friend I met recently remembered me for things that aren't even a part of my life today!

What a meaningful story the photo and the narrative make to pass on to your children!

How The Photo Scribe Will Help

The Photo Scribe will help you to work as effectively with your story as you do with your photos—cropping details, arranging the background design of family facts and history, adding in the "off-camera" elements to explain and enhance the storytelling in your album.

In photoscribing, you have two approaches for telling the complete stories of your photos.

1. You can tell the story that lies behind individual photos. In this book, you'll find techniques for uncovering and writing down the layers of details and background info the camera didn't capture. You can do this for single photographs without attempting to tell a longer, cohesive story.

For example, you have a single photo that shows all your aunts and uncles on Gran's sofa, every face beaming a smile that says "family harmony." But this was the last holiday before the argument between them kept you from seeing your cousins during your teen years. When you see that photo, you want to tell about that break and how it made you feel . . . Isn't that the story behind the photo, the one you need to write, not just the happy story the picture tells?

Sometimes I look at photos of my parents as a young couple and wonder what unrecorded story is behind the picture.

Most pictures, as time goes by, turn their stories into secrets. We know from seeing odd artifacts at yard sales that one era's familiar objects are another's curiosities. With this in mind, it is important to choose even a few pictures to photoscribe so that your personal and family history will be known and cherished in the future.

2. You can create a lifestory photo album. Captions and cameo narratives expand on individual photos, but they can do more. They can join with photos to create a story that is larger than the sum of the individual texts and photos. This greater story is told in the lifestory photo album. Striving to create a lifestory album is a more ambitious undertaking than writing individual texts but it's not beyond your abilities.

What You Won't Learn

It is **not** the aim of *The Photo Scribe* to help you to

do any of the following. This book will **not** teach you:

➤ to create a photosafe album. There are many excellent sources of information. (See the Resources Appendix, p.117) I urge you to choose photosafe materials to protect your precious photos and artifacts from deterioration. What's the point otherwise?

➤ to design page layouts. I urge you to make your albums as attractive as possible by developing a style that pleases you and expresses your taste. I caution you, however, not to allow your creativity to overpower your main purpose—to tell a story as you preserve your photos. **It's just as significant and as creatively rewarding to preserve stories as it is to preserve the images themselves.** The design and the content need to go hand in hand. *The Photo Scribe* is a scrapbooker's companion to the many layout and design books now on the market. (See Resources Appendix.)

➤ to develop long written texts. If writing appeals to you and you'd like to write more extensive family histories and personal memoirs,* be sure to check out *Turning Memories Into Memoirs, A Handbook for Writing Lifestories.* (See Soleil Press Directory, page 127.) It has helpful tips and effective exercises for writing autobiographies and memoirs. You don't need long texts, however, to create a lifestory photo album.

EXERCISE

Take a minute to think about the goals for your photo albums. Do you want to create:

➤ one or more albums in which individual cameo narratives add meaning and interest here and there (but not necessarily everywhere)?

➤ lifestory albums that are a comprehensive history of your life or your family's? This goal lets you photoscribe an autobiography or biography of any length or depth.

Good Luck

The Turning Memories™ lifewriting method has led ordinary people to become successful lifewriters for more than a decade. *The Photo Scribe* adapts Turning Memories™ techniques to album-making so that you can uncover, develop, and express *in your own words* the stories behind your photos.

You *can* succeed at writing richly detailed and interesting stories to complement your photographs and make your albums more meaningful. The work you are undertaking to photoscribe your album is important for you and for your family.

I wish you all the success and satisfaction I know you will find in photoscribing!

Points to Remember

- Your photos hold stories that are at risk of being forgotten and lost.
- Preserve your stories as written narratives as well as photos in order to convey their complexity.
- You can use photoscribing techniques to write cameo narratives for individual photos or you can weave text and photos into a unified whole to create a lifestory album—the choice is yours.
- This is *not* a book about page layout or design.
- Photoscribing is fun, fulfilling, and important!

Chapter One

Before You Begin

Many of us can speak easily and even fluently about our experiences, but when we are asked to write them down, we suddenly become wordless.

That may be one reason that photo albums are so popular. No need to struggle with writitng—the pictures say it all. Or, do they?

Photos, however interesting or well-preserved, cannot convey the meaning of your story over time. Think of the photographs in antique shops. Each unknown face that looks out at you once had a whole story—yet who tells, or knows, it now? Sure—you can see it's a wedding portrait, but were the couple in love? Did they have children? Did they live into old age together or die young? The photo is a mute remnant of a story once fully known. Without words, most of it is lost.

Each unknown face is a complete story lost, a life lived but now forgotten.

Don't despair about *your* stories getting lost. With the *The Photo Scribe,* you can learn to:

⇥ write clear, meaningful, and interesting narratives that will continue to tell your story for as long as there is someone to read it.

⇢deepen and expand the stories behind the photos in your albums by adding background information and interpretation.

⇢preserve the stories you have no pictures for but realize are so necessary for understanding who you are, who your family is.

Writing down the story behind your photographs— your lifestory or your family's—shouldn't intimidate you. Photoscribing can be as creative and as fulfilling as designing layouts or taking pictures. If you can learn to do these, you can learn to photoscribe.

Narratives in Your Photo Album

Your photo albums already have a narrative or storyline. Narrative can be told:

⇢ by the few or the many photos you've collected.

⇢ by the words you write.

⇢ by a combination of both.

Your albums, even without words, already communicate a story of your life and of your family and friends

When you know your story, you know who you are.

as they appear in the images and scenes of your photos. This image-based narrative, however, is minimal because photos can capture only a small part of any story. There are also many gaps and omissions in the stories your albums tell: the camera wasn't handy, the film was damaged, or you just forgot to take a picture. Photoscribing allows you to fill these gaps and to elaborate on the image-based narrative.

There are two narrative forms photoscribes use to create lifestory photo albums that tell the whole story.

They are the **photo caption*** and the **cameo narrative.**

1. Photo captions are the information labels placed near photos as brief phrases or bulleted lists. Captions provide the basic names and dates and serve as clues to the narrative of your story. You probably find it easy enough to write this sort of caption in your albums:

> Amy and Danny (Walden), senior prom, Central High, 1985.

When you annotate* basic info like this in an album, you assure that the basic **who, what, when,** and **where** of a photo are not lost. *The Photo Scribe* will show you how to do more: how to write an effective photo caption in your own words and how to avoid the *clichés** that seem jazzy now but convey little meaning over time. (See pp. 48-49, 85-86.)

Photographs afford us a glimpse back in history.
—Martha Stewart

2. Cameo narratives are short narratives (usually 50–150 words long) that are paired with photos or created to fill the story gap where there is no picture. A bare-bones caption adds a bit to the story your photo already tells—but not much. The larger story involves the **why** and **how,** as well as the **who, what, when, and where.** Was this a "big date" for Amy and Danny or just a pleasant social evening? Were there hopes and dreams being played out that night? Without a word-based narrative, the viewer—and that could be you in a few years—has to supply her own guesses about "prom night." She has access to none of the multiple layers of meaning that made up the unique

The story is about you.
—Horace

story of Amy and Danny that night in 1985.

When you write a narrative to go with the photo of Amy in her dress with the tiered ruffles and Danny in that dapper black tuxedo, you create a fuller, deeper account of that evening, an account that tells much more of the story as it was lived by the unique individuals who mean so much to you.

Who Are These Stories For?

Expression implies an audience—someone whose response and approval, whose cheering and appreciation we seek because sharing our lives adds to the significance of our experience. It's a fundamental human impulse to tell our stories—to someone.

Your most important audience, of course, is always yourself. Make albums of your life that please you!

Are your albums a work of self-expression (even of art)? Of course, they are! Are you preparing a photo album so you can put it away and never view it again? Not likely. Your work cries out for its audience—someone to witness the experience and insights it preserves, to applaud or to weep or to chuckle over your photos and stories.

It's wise to consider who that audience will be

Just because you write the story down doesn't mean it has to become public property.

before you photoscribe. Your audience will (and should) influence *what* you tell and *how* you tell your story. You will create a different lifestory album for your parents, for instance, than for business colleagues at your husband's promotion dinner. Being aware of who will (or may) see which album as you sort your photos and plan your project will help you make the best choices.

EXERCISE

Different albums may have different audiences. For instance, a *heritage album* may be intended for your children as adults who will be more interested in family history than they are today at age 4 and 6. A *vacation album* may have two audiences: your family this winter reliving the warmth of the holiday and your children in the future wanting to understand their childhoods. A *theme album* may have non-family members as an audience— for instance, *a career album* you may display in your office.

1. Make a list of your intended audience(s). (Jen and Jason, future grandchildren, Dave's parents, etc.)

2. Make a list of the albums you want to work on. (Diane's Friends, Florida '97, Troop #116, etc.)

3. Match the lists as appropriate. What particular needs and interests will each audience have? What will *your* needs be?

Lifestory Albums are Not Journals

When you photoscribe a lifestory album, you will always have to chose what to include and what to leave out as you record a much more detailed and complete account of your personal and family stories.

Unless you are a public figure, there is no public right to know anything about your life, present or past.

So how do you determine how deep you really want to go if your goal is to have your lifestory album(s) do more than reflect just the glossy surface of your story and yet retain privacy and dignity for yourself and for your family? Dealing with difficult stories will, after all, be very healing. (see Appendix B, "Unsettling Memories".)

Knowing from the start that there are several alter-

I don't advocate sharing everything with everyone nor turning every photo album into a lifestory album.

natives to telling everything to anyone and everyone may help you to feel more comfortable about writing down your stories. Here are suggestions on how to tell a fuller (if not always bare–your–soul complete) story to a chosen audience while maintaining privacy:

1. Create a second, slighlty different album to be kept private when your material is too personal. Create one more traditional album with brief informative captions for display. Make a duplicate lifestory album with more personal cameo narratives for you (and perhaps your family).

2. Keep cameo narratives you want to remain private in a separate companion binder or envelope. Label the separate album or envelope: *For family only: Additional narratives for lifestory photo albums.* Whether your public scrapbook has references within its pages to this private binder or envelope is up to you. (For example, next to a photo, you can write, *See pages 36-37 in Additional Family Stories Binder* or make no reference at all). When you opt for a separate binder for your more personal stories, there's no need to duplicate photos. The binder can be for stories only.

Memories are all we really own.

—Elias Lieberman

3. Take your more too-personal lifestory albums out of public view. Keep them as you would your journals—in a private place. In that way, you can be certain that they will be out of bounds to anyone with whom *you* haven't chosen to share them.

EXERCISE

Audience: Comfort vs Communication

1. Answer these questions for each era, theme or person featured in your albums. Take your time; be specific.

➠ Is there anything you don't want to share about these eras, themes, persons? Why is sharing uncomfortable to you?

➠ What info (facts and feelings/understandings) might you have a responsibility to communicate to people of the future?

2. Fill in the blanks below. Other "what if's" may occur to you as you write. Answer these too.

➠ If I told _____
about my family and their _____,
(s/he or they) would _____.

➠ If _____
knew about the time that at I _____,
it would change the way_____.

➠ If the world knew that I_____.
I would feel like I ought to _____.

3. If you keep a journal, write on the topic of your personal privacy threshold. Write for at least ten minutes.

Schedule For Success: Plan Ahead

Studies have shown that people who set specific goals—*and write them down*—accomplish more than people who don't. So I urge you to make and write down a schedule using these options:

1. Create a schedule based on hours per week. How much time do you want to devote (or can you realistically spare) for photoscribing? Be specific: "Two hours on Tuesdays and Thursdays from 9 to 11 A.M. while Emma's in pre-school" or "every weekday evening that I'm not out from 7 - 8 P.M.

2. Set a schedule based on a number of pages.
Decide how many pages you want to complete in a
week. Estimate how long it will take, then schedule that
number of hours. You'll have to
work beyond your scheduled hours if
you haven't met your page quota! Or
you could quit once you produce your
pages (but why not "bank" additional
pages for a busy week coming up?).

The photoscribing work you are doing is important to you and your family. Plan for it as you would for any important project.

**3. Set a deadline for finishing the
task.** For example, an upcoming holiday, a family
reunion, a wedding. Tell people to expect your album on
that date; their anticipation will keep you on task.

**4. Make it a rule to "pay back" time you "borrow"
before you "borrow" from your schedule again.** Like
financial debts, project debts can really add up!

Set Goals That Work For You

Photoscribing your albums may take a while! In
order to accomplish your overall goal ("to photoscribe
all my albums"), break that big goal down into intermediate ones ("to write four cameo narratives by next
Friday" or "to photoscribe my high school album by the
reunion in June"). Successfully meeting these smaller
goals will encourage you to continue as you savor your
success at regular intervals.

Keep these guidelines in mind:

1. Be realistic. Transforming your albums is a big
job. You have many photos to collect, organize, and
write about. Don't set self-defeating goals ("photoscribe
all my albums in three months").

2. Settle on a pace you can maintain. It's an important project worth doing—and so are many others! Don't preserve your past at the expense of healthfully living your present!

3. Build breaks into your work. Allow yourself to let it go for a while and then return to the task.

4. Reward yourself for accomplishing intermediate goals. Share your work with friends and family who will be appreciative. Indulge in healthy "treats."

5. Don't force yourself to write about difficult times. Eras, people, or events you don't want to deal with don't have to be your first subjects. There may be some years you really don't want to document—at least not yet. Focus first on subjects that will bring the most satisfaction. You'll find difficult or sad times easier to write about if you learn the skills and experience the satisfaction by photoscribing happy times first! (See Appendix B for more information on dealing with unsettling memories.)

Mother was amazed. She had no idea what I meant when I told her I was photoscribing. When she saw the album I made about Grandma and Grandpa, she choked up. She was so pleased that I cared.

6. Be selective. You don't have to write a narrative for every photo in an album.

7. Share your work-in-progress. Show it to supportive friends and family. Let their enthusiasm inspire you. But don't depend on others—praise *yourself* for work you both accomplish and plan.

8. Establish the habit of organizing your photos as they come in. Label new photos right away to avoid turning today's photos into tomorrow's mystery pictures. Keep a notebook for details and impressions.

9. Use a binder to organize your photoscribing

project-in-process. Keep rough drafts, exercises, lists, and notes in a three-ring binder with dividers for each category. (The *Photo Scribe's Memory Binder* is designed just for this. See the Soleil Press Directory, page 127.)

Photosafe is Photosmart

If you're going to preserve your photographs, invest in photo-safe materials that will last. Do it once, do it for good! Why create an album whose pages will destroy your photos—and your creative work—within a generation? (See the Resources Appendix.)

Can you afford *not* to record your personal and family history? It is one of your most valuable assets, and an invaluable gift to give to the future.

Points to Remember

- Photoscribe your stories.
- Captions and cameo narratives expand on your photos and bridge the gaps between them.
- Audience influences your choice of what to write.
- Photoscribing doesn't mean making your private life public—how much you share is your choice.
- Make yourself a schedule. Plan it, share it with others, and then stick to it!
- Set realistic goals.
- Photo-safe is always photosmart. It's worth the effort and expense to use materials that will last.

Chapter Two

The Lifelist

The life you (or your family or subject) **have lived, not the photos you have available,** is the organizing principle behind creating a lifestory photo album.

Writing cameo narratives that tell the story behind the photos of a lifetime and that fill in the gaps in your collection can be daunting—even when you're still relatively young. What you need is a guide that will make the task "doable." The Lifelist* is such a guide. It will take you through the process of photoscribing your lifestory albums.

A Lifelist is a list of everything and anything you've ever done, said, thought, or felt, and of everyone and everything you've ever known in your life.

"Oh, my goodness," I can hear you saying. "You've got to be kidding—*everything?!!*"

Now don't panic and don't dismiss the idea before reading on. The Lifelist is a tool that will actually simplify your photoscribing process while it deepens the level of meaning in your albums.

Your Lifelist, whatever its type, must contain many detailed memories, of little as well as significant events and relationships.

Creating your Lifelist will help you to:

•• **remember and record your life in more detail.**

•• **identify and prioritize events and interactions** of your life, in order to record or feature them in your lifestory photo album.

Photoscribing without a Lifelist is like setting out on a journey without a map or any directions.

•• **help you fill gaps in photos** with interesting and well-written cameo narratives.

•• **determine the story you tell** rather than let the story be dictated by the photos you happen to have. Your story should be enhanced, rather than limited, by your photos.

How To Compile Your Lifelist

The secret to success in compiling a Lifelist is to write down everything that goes through your head. No kidding! Don't judge. Don't evaluate. Just keep writing down everything that pops into your head.

A Lifelist starts with slowing down your thoughts and allowing yourself to remember.

Making a lifestory album is a journey inward to your self and then outward to your family.

Let your thoughts wander. Jot down whatever memories come up. Write without reservation and just long enough to recall the memory clearly—as few as 3 to 5 words may be enough. Remembering or writing chronologically is not necessary.

Here are topics that appear on Lifelists:

•• early childhood memories

•• first schooling

•• the arrival of a sibling

→ the community (town, street), the ethnic or religious group you grew up in

→ fires, floods, tornadoes, accidents, or other mishaps

→ family illnesses, deaths

→ important or influential relationships with relatives, an elder, or a peer

→ failures or successes at high school, scholarships, a decision to go or not to go to the university, a conflict with a teacher, having to leave school for work

EXAMPLES
from my lifelist circa 1963
→ annual ice festival
→ very serious about studying
→ using the language lab
→ binding books in the library
→ silence in the study halls
→ mail call at 10:40 AM
→ walking outside after classes
→ honor roll: 80 or better
→ ships docking downtown
→ learning Spanish
→ early winter darkness
→ emphasis on team sports
→ lights from the mill

→ boyfriends / girlfriends, deciding to marry or not

→ career, training, work life, achievements

→ friendships, colleagues

→ home life, house life, family life, your children

Your list will eventually get longer and more detailed. It will even contain specific memories of a particular day or experience as well as more general memories of things you did and experienced many times. Under "childhood memories," you might write something like: *sitting on the green chair next to Mother; molasses cookies; picking apples at Grandma's;* and *summers at the lake* .

People sometimes wonder if a certain memory is important enough to be included on a Lifelist. Don't worry if a certain memory is important or not. If you think of it,

As you compile your Lifelist, memories will be jumbled—old ones next to new, important ones next to trivial. That's ok for now. Sorting is a separate, later task.

Photoscribing with a Lifelist will help you to write what you want to write: no need to worry if you've missed a turn or spent hours on the wrong road!

it's definitely important enough to go on your Lifelist. All your memories are important; all of them can be used in some way to inform (or give background to) successful and interesting narratives that you will tell in photo and text.

EXERCISE

1. Write down at least twenty memories (forty would be better, and eighty preferable) for your Lifelist. Use just 3 to 5 words for each. Write and remember uncritically. Chronology is not important at this stage.

2. Place this list in a binder for reference.

Lifelists—Long and Short

When you record memories of an entire lifetime on your Lifelist, you are producing an **Extended Lifelist.*** My example (p.29) is an

The more memories, the more choice when you use the Lifelist as a map to photoscribe your albums.

excerpt from my Extended Lifelist. Eventually, it has several hundred or even as many as five hundred or more items. It's not unusual for people who are reviewing their entire lives to devote time over two or three weeks to this one task alone.

When doing a particular album, it's not always necessary to compile an Extended Lifelist. Sometimes a short list is needed. It's called the **Limited Lifelist.***

➦Do you want to work on an album of just one period (Zach's infancy), event (Mira's wedding), or theme (Bob's volunteer work) of your life or of the life of another person? When you create a Lifelist for one album—or even for several pages, you are generating a Limited Lifelist.

➥ You may also want to elaborate parts of an Extended Lifelist into smaller, more detailed memories. When

you focus on a smaller category of time, place, subject or event, you are creating a Limited Lifelist.

Let's look at the last topic on the Lifelist (your children) on page 29. Here's how you might elaborate to focus on the birth of your second child in a Limited Lifelist:

➥ recalled conversations with older child about the baby brother/sister to come

➥ preparations (be specific: clothes, crib, the first-born's bedtime routine)

➥ classes, pre-natal care and care-givers, baby shower, friends/relatives

➥ the birth day itself, special details, the story

➥ reactions/adaptations from older child

Now you have a map of this topic. Use it as a guide to tell the story in photos and narratives. Notice that you have not yet worked with photos. Remember: it is important to work with your memories *before* you work with your photos. Memory—your memory—is

Step One in creating a complete lifestory album. Referring to your photos is Step Two.

EXERCISE

1. Choose one item from the Extended Lifelist you have begun.

2. Make a Limited Lifelist: write down on a separate paper as many as ten *specific* component memories that you associate with that one general memory.

For instance, if you wrote *high school graduation*, now write: ✓Aunt Lil came for Baccalaureate ✓Mom had the flu that week ✓Nancy came from D.C. ✓Posey's party ✓Wilma's chocolate cake ✓daisy chain ✓my gown was too short, ✓Uncle Leo's call, ✓gifts from Marianne.

Keep at it!

Once you start actively recalling memories for a Lifelist, you will find that they surface at all sorts of moments: while you wait for a traffic light to turn, while you gaze out the window as you do the dishes, while you chat at a friend's house about your week.

Memories surface from the unconscious. When you forget something, it's because your unconscious has swallowed it up. The unconscious yields a memory only reluctantly—and snatches it back as quickly as possible. That's why we forget.

To create a lifestory album, you must first know your story and all its details.

Beat the unconscious: carry a small spiral notebook around in your pocket or purse to jot down memories as they come back to you. That way you won't forget—your memory will be in writing.

After a while your Extended or even your Limited Lifelist may seem long. Don't quit just yet! In fact, it's probably not long enough yet! Continue to add to it in the days and months ahead as more memories occur to you. Placed in your *Photo Scribe Memory Binder* with your narratives, your list helps organize your lifestory album. (See Soleil Press Directory, page 127.)

EXERCISE

1. Review your Extended Lifelist.

2. On separate pieces of paper, make a Limited Lifelist for each of the topics that interest you. As you come across memories that belong to another topic, put them on that page.

3. Work with these lists to make them useful. Add, delete, combine or expand until you are satisfied. Some photoscribes focus on one topic or era at a time; others enjoy multitasking this Lifelist process. Either way, the Lifelist you create will assure that you maintain the storyline you want to preserve.

Memory Is Often Faulty

You may feel that you already know your story—after all, you are the one who has lived your life! The fact is most of us don't really remember our stories—not even the ones we are so sure we remember well. What we "know" is a version that has evolved over the years through remembering and feeling. There is a lot to be said for the theory that we remember the memory (the last time we remembered) and not the event!

> *Memory is a very frail thing. The written word stands forever.*
> —M. Ghandi

Those of us old enough to have lived through the assassination of John Kennedy often say—and certainly believe it—that "people can never forget where they were when they heard that Kennedy was shot."

One fall, I took the occasion of the anniversary of Kennedy's murder to tell my children when and where I had learned about it. Later, in the process of writing about memory, I went back to my journal entry.

Neither the time that I remembered when I had learned of the assassination nor the place I had thought I was in was correct according to my journal entry which I wrote just days after the event! It's a study in itself to ponder how we recreate our selves and self-images by subtly altering our memories over time.

Don't assume that your memory is reliable. Always cross-check your Lifelist facts for corroboration.

EXERCISE

A. If you are a journal keeper, you can easily confirm the faulty memory phenomenon:

1. Recall an incident that occurred at least ten years ago.

2. Write down the details as you remember them.

3. Cross check your memories by going back to the journal where you recorded the incident; compare what you wrote then with what you've written now.
I am confident that you will find some, perhaps even many, discrepancies in the two versions.

B. If you are not a journal keeper,

1. Follow steps 1 and 2 above.

2. Then cross check your memories by:
- ⇨ **Rereading old letters, newspaper clippings, diplomas, or other artifacts you may have.**
- ⇨ **Asking others who were there what details they remember.**

3. Now compare what you learned from your research with what you first wrote. Does new or different information suggest that you should revise your list or account?

Points to Remember

•◆ Compile your Lifelist uncritically. It is your basic tool for remembering and organizing a lifestory album.

•◆ Work with your memories first and your photographs second.

•◆ Lifelists can be Extended or Limited.

•◆ Memory isn't always as accurate as we think. Verify names, dates, and details in a variety of ways.

Note to workshop leaders and teachers: The worksheet, Writing Great Cameo Memory Lists, *provides an extensive step–by–step exercise for developing a Lifelist. It greatly facilitates the task of teaching this aspect of photoscribing. Please refer to the Soleil Press Directory for info (page 126).*

Chapter Three

Working with Photographs

Your next step in making a lifestory album is to work with your photos. In this chapter, you will:

1. Get to know your photos. Doing so will make it easier to write the stories behind them.

2. Expand your Lifelist. It's time to let your pictures stimulate your memory so that you keep adding to your Lifelist.

3. Determine where the gaps are in your photo collection. You will fill these with additional photos or cameo narratives.

Starting Points

Although you can start a lifestory photo album from anywhere on your Lifelist or in your photo collection, good choices for a beginner include:

➫ **the last six months.** Events and details are fresh in your mind so documenting and cross-checking them will be easy. With details under control, you can practice the skills of creating a lifestory album.

➫ **a distinct era for which you have few photos.** The photo selec-

Your memories and thoughts about specific photos and your Lifelist are the tools you will use to write both photo captions and cameo narratives.

tion process is minimal, and it is more evident and pressing to fill out the story line with words instead of photos.

➡ **a period that has little emotional impact for you.** You may be afraid of the feelings associated with some photos. By working first with neutral images and unchallenging memories, you can learn the skills you need without confronting difficult content.

➡ **a year for which you already have written material.** The process is more accessible when you use existing journal entries, letters, or vignettes* and stories that you have on hand.

➡ **an event such as a wedding, graduation, or retirement.** These can present a clearly defined focus.

Grouping Your Photos

Your photos are an important source of memories. They will help you fill out your Lifelist.

1. Group your photos in some way that makes sense to you. There are many ways you can do this:

➡ **by occasion** (Thanksgiving 1996)

➡ **by subject** (Troop 101, '96-'97)

➡ **by time period** (Max's baby photos)

➡ **by character** (Nana McGowan)

I was amazed at how many details and little moments from my past came back to me when I spent more time dwelling with my photos!

Sometimes as you group your photos like this, memories that hadn't surfaced earlier will at this point. Jot down these new memories on your Lifelist. (Remember not to censor any thoughts or feelings.)

2. Dwell with the events and eras of your "go-together" photos.

Simply linger with the photos. Look at them intently; stay with each photo or with groups of them. Additional memories and feelings may arise. Record these on your Lifelist.

3. Go through your Lifelist and note which memories do not appear in any photographs. These cameo narrative topics will deepen and complement your other pictures.

It can be frustrating to complete your album and then discover photos that could deepen and, in some cases, alter a story in the album.

4. Ask family and friends for copies of photos you don't have but wish you did. Record in your Lifelist any memories that arise.

EXERCISE

1. Surround yourself with photos of a period from which you want to recall more—or more detailed—memories. In your home, office, or wherever you spend large amounts of time, set them where you can see them daily: in a line on a table in your living room, tucked into a picture frame in the kitchen, resting on a lamp on your bureau.

2. As you look at these photos, you will find yourself remembering what you see in the photo itself: "Oh, yes, my grandfather had that habit of always. . ." or "my mother wore that green winter coat forever."

These are "old" memories. By recalling them, however, you set the stage for remembering other details: how your father would say, "Nancy, go out and get a new coat" and how she would reply, "It's good enough to go another year." Suddenly, you remember how it wasn't just over the coat that your parents would quibble like this. As you allow this photo to evoke these familiar voices, you leave the "old" memories and find yourself in "new" ones. When you linger with your photos, you enter their world and remember things suggested by, but not specifically in, the photos you hold in your hand.

3. Add these memories to your Lifelist.

Personally Speaking

When working with photos from my past, I have often come across overlooked or forgotten elements.

In a photo of myself at about three sitting on the steps of my grandparents' house with my brother, my mother squints into the sunlight. One day, I suddenly saw my grandmother's smiling face emerge from the background.*. What had been a shadow is a doting grandmother. Behind the posed foreground,* the spontaneous snapshot is one I have come to treasure. "Oops," she says to me these many years later with a happy expression not captured in other photos I have of her, "I didn't mean to walk into the picture!"

Because I lingered with this photo, I discovered my

grandmother in the background. This led me to many memories about her style of grandmothering.

By lingering with two other pictures, I caught a mistake in dates. There is a child wearing the same winter suit in these two shots. The child in the first is clearly me. The second photo is a bit indistinct. Looking again, I wonder innocently why I don't look more like myself. Then I ask myself why I'm an infant in the picture with my mother in front of the house on Webster Street—we moved there when I was three.

Then it clicks! I was certain—but wrong because I ignored the evidence. It is my younger sister in my outgrown outfit. *She* was the baby when we lived in that house. How could I have placed this photo next to another of myself taken two years earlier?

EXERCISE

I. Choose a number of photos of one period or with one theme (at least five). Scrutinize them for answers to the following questions. Jot down the answers for future use.

➥ What do the *backgrounds* in the photos tell us about the people in the photos?

➥ What are their *income levels?* their *tastes?* their *educations?* their *religious practices?*

➥ What do the things you see in the photograph tell you about *daily life?* Be sure to take into account such features as dress, shoes, eyeglasses, pets, yards, cars, neighborhoods, toys.

➥ Are there members of the family or other *people missing from the photos* who, you think should be there? Why are they are not there?

➥ By *the way people are standing together or apart*, turned toward or away from each other, can you "see" something significant about their relationships?

2. Be a detective: look at each photo and ask any and every question. What happened before and after the photo was taken? Why did these people come together for this occasion?

3. Search for hidden elements you had not noticed before even in recent photograph. Also ask yourself what the photos would tell you about yourself if you were a stranger looking at them.

4. Note your feelings that emerge from viewing these photos. How do they inform you about yourself or the people shown?

5. Repeat this exercise and use your "new eyes" to find the hidden elements in every photo you include in your lifestory photo album. Choose a number of photos of one period or with one theme. (Be sure to select at least five.) Scrutinize these photos for answers to the above questions. Have a pad of paper handy to jot down your answers for future reference.

Points to Remember

•◦ Choose an era or an event that makes a workable starting point.

•◦ Group your photos to stimulate your memory. Dwell with your groups of photos for a while— then add your thoughts, feeling and memories to your Lifelist.

•◦ Don't rush! Allow yourself the time to linger with the process.

Chapter Four

Writing great Captions

Now that you've generated (at least part of) your Lifelist and have grouped your photos, it's time to start writing the text for your lifestory album(s).

A photoscribe's two basic writing tools are the **caption** and the **cameo narrative.** While longer autobiographical essays can be effective in albums or as separate books (and I encourage you to write full memoirs if this interests you), this book doesn't address that process. (See *Turning Memories Into Memoirs*, Soleil Press Directory.) Full-length memoirs, however, are *not* necessary for a lifestory album.

Just a Few Words

Captions are identifications or brief tags that you write to accompany your photos. They are essential to your albums because they establish:

•❖a **"cast of characters"***: mother, grandfather, your children as babies, friends. (Identifications are important since appearances change.)

•❖**an action (plot)***: a wedding or a graduation (when neither the bride nor the graduate are in the photo, what clue is there to make the occasion clear, years later, when you look at the photo of smiling, well-dressed people?)

➤ **a setting***: this city and not that city; this year, not that year; this event, not that event; this cultural

background and not that one. (Again, will such distinctions be identifiable years from now?)

Remember that captions provide the following information as they furnish character, action, setting:

➤ *Who* **is in the photo? Include full names and relationships of characters to each other and to you:** *Aunt Mary (Donaldson), my mother's sister.*

➤ *What* **is portrayed in the photo? Include both action and setting of the occasion and any background description:** *wedding reception for Stephanie (Mary's daughter).*

Here you can also include extra information: *Aunt Mary made Steph's wedding gown.*

➤ *Where* **(in what setting) does the action occur? Include names of buildings, streets, cities:** *at the Knights of Columbus Hall, Grand Rapids, Michigan.*

➤ *When* **is the event occurring? This is setting and it refers to the time. Include year, date and day as appropriate:** *Saturday, June 23, 1973.*

What else was going on (action) in the family or the individual's life: *Aunt Mary was recovering from the heart attack she'd had in April.*

Finished captions do not separate the basic elements as I do above to illustrate this point. Because I wanted to make clear the distinctions of **who, what,**

where, and **when**, I wrote separate sentences for each. For an album, I would write these into one caption:

> Aunt Mary (O'Connell Donaldson), my mother's sister, at her daughter Stephanie's (Martin) wedding reception, Knights of Columbus Hall, Grand Rapids, Saturday, June 23, 1973. Although she was recovering from a heart attack, she made Steph's wedding gown, including the embroidery on the bodice.

The information in this "Aunt Mary caption" is important and should be included on an album page, but the details needn't be featured with every photo or even with every cluster of photos of that event. You don't need to repeatedly identify Aunt Mary on subsequent pages (but you should label the back of each and every picture with a photo-safe pencil in case it is ever separated from the album).

If a number of years have passed since someone last appeared in your album, it's best to identify them. Your kids, not as familiar with Aunt Mary as you are, may not recognize her at a different time of her life.

EXERCISE

1. Select a page of your album or a few photos.

2. Write captions that provide the *who, what, where,* **and** *when* **that pertain to each photo.**

3. As you do so, write specific, proper words: "Aunt Mary" not "an aunt"; "the Knights of Columbus Hall, Grand Rapids, MI" not "a rented hall." For another photo, you might write "Popham Beach" not "at the shore"; "3rd grade at Marion T. Morse School" not "early school years."

As they go through your albums, your family and friends should be able to trace your life from person to person, from place to place, from time to time. Be clear and specific with your information in order to preserve the whole story.

Tips for Writing Captions

In an album, the basic **who, what, where,** and **when** captions are essential for identifying people, places and things. Captions, even short ones, can also provide opportunities to:

➛**write from the heart.** Write the words that say what you feel! Let yourself be poetic and romantic. Let your imagination soar!

I remember spending hours just looking at you when you were a new baby. It felt like we were still one and my whole life was brand new just like you.

➛**write with candor.** Just say it. Let yourself write what you want to write. Express all your love and admiration, your hopes and under-standings, your thoughts and your experience.

People would always stop to talk with him when we went into town. He was very well-liked. Everyone knew him. He was a different person in town than at home, where he spent hours in his study, alone.

➛**write with details.** Use your senses. Describe a sight, a taste, a sound, a smell, the feel of something in the photo in specific details.

My task... is, by the power of the written word, to make you hear, to make you feel— it is, before all, to make you see. That, and no more, and it is everything.
—Joseph Conrad

The rain scattered the glowing red and yellow leaves across the slippery black road. As we walked we could smell frost-bitten, rotting leaves and the wet pavement smell of autumn.

➛**write simply.** Don't go looking for big words. The vocabulary you have right now is just fine. There's no need to try to be fancy or deep.

Sometimes the surface is all right because it's surface you need to tell.

> We left at 10 P.M. and by 7:30 the next morning, we were at Linda's eating breakfast at her kitchen table overlooking the lake.

•❖ **write your impressions.** Photo captions are your chance to express your "take" on life itself and on your life and your family's in particular.

> Those were our happiest years. It seemed like we were all working on the same thing for the same purpose. I'd go back to those days anytime!

EXERCISE

1. Review albums you have previously created and evaluate at least 10 captions.

2. Rewrite them, if necessary, asking yourself if you have written:

✓from the heart ✓with candor ✓with details ✓with simplicity
✓with your impressions.

Problem Captions

While captions present you with many opportunities to make an effective album, they can also drag your albums down if you're not aware of potential problems. These can include:

1. meaningless prose that fills space without much thought. You might be tempted to write for photos of an ocean vacation, *The ocean was so beautiful!*

While you might say, "But, that's how I feel. The ocean *was* beautiful!" there is much more feeling and experience to explore and share. For instance, **how** does the ocean make you feel: rested or restless, centered or isolated, connected to the universe or uneasy? **What** affects you: the sound, the light, color, the move-ment of the waves, the open space?

Avoid meaningless writing by taking the time to linger with your photos. Re-enter the time when the pictures were taken, and recall the feelings and features of your life at that time.

In writing a caption for that ocean photo, ask yourself questions like: "What did this vacation mean to me?" or "How was I specifically affected by being in that place at that time?" As a result of these and similar questions, you might write one of the two captions that follow in your album:

> Jan and I were finally able to drop our roles as business partners and be a couple again in those two weeks at Monhegan.

> As a water sign, I found being at the ocean restored and revived me in a way that other places—mountains and forests—don't.

2. borrowed phrases. These predictable, uninfor-mative, and generally uninteresting tags are also called *clichés*. For instance, for a photo of you working in the garden why write a flippant caption like:

- ➔ *A girl's work is never done!*
- ➔ *Where's the sun block?!*
- ➔ *I love to get my hands dirty.*
- ➔ *Oh, my nails!*

The slightly mocking voice of a stranger is an album convention from the past that doesn't serve the photoscribe well.

Think of yourself ten years from now looking at the photo of you working in the garden. (Even more, imagine your grown children in twenty years!) What will flippant captions say about who you were and what you were doing? What can cute captions contribute to the making of a lifestory photo album? Not much!

Every caption you write in your albums can be interesting, meaningful, and satisfying to read—and re-read as you return to them again and again. All it takes is attention to detail and a commitment to the future (qualities you already have or you wouldn't be reading this book!).

Clichés will never tell you or your children's children the story behind the photograph.

Now think of your garden photo annotated with something like this:

> Last year I began composting all our kitchen and yard waste and the garden absolutely bloomed! It was my best garden to date.

or

> I enjoyed gardening that summer and I was good at it (note the five different types of lettuce lower right)!

3. repeated information already in the photo. For a picture of your kids in a treehouse, why write: *The kids at the treehouse.* Instead, use the opportunity to say something, in your own words, about these wondrously unique kids of yours that is not already obvious from the picture:

> As usual, Kylie had big plans and Ryan kept calling out cautions. Kylie liked working alone while Ryan wanted to work with Papa.

> Kylie and Ryan have very different play styles, but they were able to work well on this project! They played in the treehouse all summer.

Imagine your grandchildren, years from now, reading the two treehouse captions. Which will be more satisfying to them because it tells them more?

➤ When what is going on in the photo is not

entirely obvious, then stating it clearly in the caption is in order. Fabric spread out on a table doesn't say what is being cut out or why. *Making shower curtains for the new bathroom* then becomes an important piece of information. It's not just repeating the photo because the activity is not obvious from the picture by itself.

4. jokes. While an album certainly doesn't have to be serious in a gloomy way, I encourage you not to

Strive to be a family historian not a stand-up comic in your albums.

weigh it down with jokes that are probably doomed to lose meaning over time. Humor often depends largely on awareness of contemporary, often mass, culture. Once the references are obsolete (cartoon characters, TV shows and personalities are made to be replaced), how can anyone in the future "get it?" (For instance, I remember the 1960s icon Bobby Dylan vividly. His raspy voice is instantly recognizable to me, but not to my kids. A joke about sounding like Dylan is meaningless to them. Why include it in my album?)

➻ Will a "witty" reference to a character in a Brad Pitt movie mean anything to your grandkids in 2020?

➻ Will Madonna still be a star so that your grandchildren will chuckle at your quip under the photo of their mother, age four, in dress-up clothes?

➻ Some cultural icons will, of course, survive. Jaws or ET, Jurassic Park and Star Wars may be familiar to yet another generation. But since you can, why not make your album an original statement, one *in your own words* rather than a borrowed statement? In a photo of your son swimming towards his sister, why waste the opportunity by writing *Here comes Jaws!* Why not write: *Matthew was always trying to surprise*

Amy, and she was always dunking him. This was how he learned to swim! Honestly, which caption tells more about your children and which will prompt more memories when you read it in 20 years?

By Hand or By Key?

If you don't already have a preference about how to record your captions in your albums, you might consider these options for balancing the two goals of legibility and preserving the artifact of your handwriting (as well as giving your albums the personal touch of hand lettering):

➥ **write just the captions by hand and type your longer cameo narratives.**

➥ **do both—write everything by hand and also type at least some of your texts.** This gives the reader a choice of which to read if you combine them in one book, or gives you a text-only version to store.

➥ **write a few entries or headlines by hand and type the rest.**

Your goal is to make the stories of your life and those of your family accessible. Handwriting can be difficult to decipher—not just because of poor penmanship but because handwriting styles change and what was once easy to read can become difficult. *How do you want to be remembered?* Reading handwritten text can be tiring and unappealing. If they are illegible, your family stories may effectively be lost!

Points to Remember

- ◆ Captions establish a cast of **characters**, a **plot** and a **setting** for your lifestory album. Captions tell your audience the **who, what, when** and **where** of your lifestory.
- ◆ Although it may be tempting to rely on borrowed phrases, *clichés*, or trendy captions as a kind of shorthand, future generations will appreciate most the captions written **in your own words**.
- ◆ Bring details into your captions—be specific by describing particular **sights, tastes, smells, sounds, textures** and **feelings**.
- ◆ You can either write your captions by hand or use a word processor—there are pros and cons to both.

Chapter Five

Writing Great Cameo Narratives

The cameo narrative, after the Lifelist, is your most important photoscribing tool—whether you are creating a lifestory album or simply telling more of the story behind an individual photo. Cameo narratives are longer than captions and contain more "ingredients," but they remain relatively short texts—generally 50 to 150 words.

Compared to captions, cameo narratives:

- **furnish many more details.** They complete what is either not apparent or else not visible in the photo. Unlike short captions, cameos reveal much more than core information.

- **provide more space to tell your story.** The whole story is more than names, dates and locales.

When I go through my albums, it makes me happy. I really have a lovely family!

- **stand in for photos.** When no pictures are available to document an item on your Lifelist, the cameo narrative is essential to tell the story.

- **contribute many more rich textures of feeling and life experience by adding *why* and *how*.** Life is complex and multi-layered, and your albums can be, too! *Why* and *how* are often too complex to include in short captions and certainly beyond the power of a photograph to convey on its own. (If your goal is to create a lifestory album, you can't do it without portraying that complexity. You need cameo narratives.)

Writing Guidelines

You can help yourself to write great cameo narratives by following these steps:

1. Study your go-together photos. Place these photos together with your Lifelist in front of you. Group photos with items on your list and give this grouping a title. (For the time being, I'll direct you to work with cameo narratives that complement photos.)

What are you feeling or thinking as you look at the photos or read the items on your Lifelist? What comes to mind immediately? Make notes on your Lifelist of these feelings and thoughts as you experience them.

2. Write the important stuff. Ask yourself: what's crucial about this photo (these photos)? Then write what you most want people to know—facts and details you want them to remember. Trust your intuition. Often the first thought that comes to mind is the most important. Don't worry about style, grammar, or whether your writing's good enough. Editing is a later step.

My kids have grown up in the South. They've never had frozen mittens or seen blue shadows across a snowy field. I want them to get the feel of that from my album.

3. Write as short or long a piece as you want to. If you write 20 words, your rough draft will become a caption, not a cameo narrative, but that's not a problem. Just place this text in your album *as a caption*. What's important is using text to bring more meaning to your photos.

If you write 50 to 150 words, your text will become a cameo narrative. You may find that what you've written is not enough (or too much) and you'll change the text of your cameo. Keeping yourself open to this process helps you produce the best cameo narratives you are capable of writing.

Too much happens in one life to write it all down. Choose what tells the story best.

4. Keep each cameo narrative focused on one person, idea, setting, or action. If you want to write something else about that person, idea, setting, or action, draft a new cameo narrative on a separate page with its own title or heading. A story within a story can be confusing. The reader gets lost trying to follow the storyline. Let each story stand on its own.

5. Write in short, simple sentences. Don't worry about being fancy as you put ideas and words together. Simple is often best. Keeping sentences short helps you write clearly. It's not true that complicated writing has more meaning!

After a dozen words, look for a way to end your sentence. After twenty, end it! Cameo narratives and captions should not be long and rambling.

6. Let cameo narratives be independent pieces of writing if necessary. Cameo narratives can be placed by themselves in your lifestory albums—they don't have to be connected to a photo or to another cameo narrative. They can be about a memory on your Lifelist that isn't preserved in a photo. The connection of these "stand alone" cameos to your photos is an inherent one—the life you have lived.

Topics for Cameos

What sorts of topics are appropriate for you to write about in your cameo narratives? Here's a list to use to get you thinking about different possibilities:

1. The reason for the photograph. Why are these people together and what impact did the event have on them? Include information about what led up to the moment pictured. This sort of cameo narrative can serve as a broad statement about your family or your life. An appropriate cameo narrative next to a photo of a woman in her mid-forties might be:

Paint a word picture to introduce your elders and old-time friends honestly and lovingly to your family of today and of the future.

After the kids were grown, I was ready to work outside the home. Randall was tired after his twenty five years at DuPont and eager for a less hurried pace. Once I started looking, a job just fell in my lap as a graphic designer. Randall took responsibility of the house and kept a few accounts as a consultant. "It feels like when we were first together," he told me one day.

2. Particulars about the event or setting that are not obvious from the photo. Your cameo narratives can record details that shaped or affected the event or setting that was photographed. Include clothing, words, props, interesting or unusual physical features.

Nana was very proud of her mantlepiece and loved to decorate it for holidays. One year Pops ordered flowers to be delivered in time for the dinner. She was so pleased . . .

3. "Portraits" of the people in the photo. There are two kinds of portraits you can include:

➺**Physical portraits.** Although the people portrayed in your albums are familiar to you, people you've loved and known, they are often unfamiliar to your children and grandchildren. Your family may not know what certain relatives looked like beyond a head shot or a picture of them in a group. Captions present names, relationships, and dates, while cameo narratives do more—they present the whole person.

> Daddy's grandmother, Anya Magyar, was tall—about five foot ten—and heavy-set. Her hands and fingers were strong and broad from having worked in the fields for years. Her long, white hair was always in a bun at the back of her head. When I first met her, she looked me right in the eye and said, "Welcome to our family." She had a strong Hungarian accent.

➺**Character portraits.** Create windows on your characters' inner lives by giving your audience glimpses of how they felt, why they felt that way, and what they thought. You may have to simply tell us how you suppose your characters felt and thought— and be sure you attribute your guess work to yourself or to another person. Often guesses can be made more plausible by referring to conversations and actions of your characters.

> "Boy, that was a day!" Greg said after his first day of work at the studio. He was so full of energy; I could see he had found something new and important. "This is it!" he said, clasping his hands. It was lovely to watch his eagerness. He'd been looking for a challenge and was so happy to have found one.

4. Dialogue.* Including conversations allows us to hear people's voices as you once heard them. Dialogue is so important that the entire next chapter is devoted to it.

Dialogue allows us to hear the voices of loved ones speaking across the years.

5. Settings in which people lived. A setting is the environment in which your characters live and in which the action of the picture occurs. The setting includes *the place* (geography, buildings, interiors), *the time* (year, month, day, hour), and *the atmosphere* (mood, feeling, ethnic culture, religion, educational levels, etc.). Setting is crucial for interpreting character. It is often the most inaccessible element for your younger readers. This is unfortunate since setting is an element they will need in order to understand the story you tell in your album.

To convey setting, write portraits of houses and neighborhoods, landscapes, geographic regions, eras, seasons, and events. Culture, ethnic heritage, social, political and even labor history can also be part of the setting for your cameo narratives.

> Our house (at 18 Spring Street) was three blocks from Westin Elementary—close enough for Jamie to walk. Maples formed a canopy over the street. On autumn mornings, Jamie shuffled though the leaves—they were six inches thick on the sidewalk. The old man who lived at the corner always had a huge pile of leaves. I think he liked seeing the kids have fun and made piles just for them! Jamie and his friend Sam would take a running leap and throw themselves into the pile on their way to school. More than once, I got a call from the school because Jamie was late. The perfect leap into that pile of leaves was too tempting!

In describing a place, start with where you are standing (actually or in your imagination) and describe everything you can see from east to west, left to right, or top to bottom. Determine an order that makes sense and follow it.

> Behind Jill is Mt. James blocking out the horizon. Behind her is Eagle Lake.

It's very shallow and fish swim close to the surface. From where she stood, you can see . . .

In describing a period or a culture simply write your reactions as you might in a letter or diary. (By "culture," I mean the customs and habits of a given era, region, family, generation, or institution as well as the more familiar "culture" as ethnic customs.) For instance, "In those days, people wore —" Don't presume such information is too obvious or even uninteresting to today's (and tomorrow's) audience; it paints a portrait of the time and place. If you have traveled abroad you know how fascinating the most mundane things can be— grocery packaging, for instance, in a foreign language. Your audience will be interested in the "foreign" cultures in your photos. "Why is Grandma doing that?" a child may ask, unaware that everyone did that then (a recent memory for you but pre-history for your kids, so be sure you explain!)

The culture of your childhood and youth may be as foreign to your children or grandchildren as the culture of Outer Mongolia!

EXERCISE

1. Choose a photo of a person.

2. Portray that person's character by writing about some action that shows his or her character.

3. Now describe the setting your character lived in. This can be your subject's community, ethnic origins, religion, or all three plus other similar kinds of setting details.

4. Combine the two—character and setting— to create one cameo narrative.

5. Now reread your portrait. Can you add more details, clarify a point, or add a sensory detai?. Place the reworked piece in your *Photo Scribe Memory Binder*.

Points to Remember

- Because cameo narratives are longer than captions, they can do a better job of completing the photos and fill in the story gaps between them.
- Follow this chapter's suggested guidelines to write your cameo narratives.
- Topics for your cameo narratives vary. Your album will be more interesting if you also vary the formats of your cameo narratives.

Note to workshop leaders and teachers: The instructional worksheet, Writing Great Cameo Narratives, offers a step–by–step process for photoscribes to develop cameo narratives. Please refer to the Soleil Press Directory for info (page 126).

Chapter Six

Giving Voice to Photographs

Writing dialogue for the people who appear in your photos brings your lifestory album "characters" to life. It's important to let your children *hear* the voices of those who came before them. When I use *voice** in this context, I mean not just the sound but the whole personality and character that produced it. More than just the words spoken by someone, voice is the meaning and the significance behind those words in their life and yours. In giving voice to your characters, you will always be striving to record more than the actual words they spoke.

Habits of speech are unique characteristics that tell us about our ancestors and ourselves.

As a family historian, a photoscribe necessarily interprets the past as choices are made about what to write.

Narrative with dialogue is stronger and more energetic than narrative without it. For example, which of the following cameos allows us to feel Myra's presence and to hear her speaking across the years?

Cameo Without Dialogue:

When Myra returned from Italy, we picked her up at the airport. She was very excited. She had decided to take art classes at the Institute. That was the beginning of her flamboyant new "career" as an artist.

61

Cameo With Dialogue:

"It made me want to paint again, visiting all those fabulous churches in Italy. It was absolutely overwhelming—the colors, the light, the marble! I just can't go back to the office and have no connection to those paintings. Life is too short! I've decided to start at the Institute as soon as the new term begins."

EXERCISE

1. Choose a photo of two people. Remember a conversation between them or a typical exchange. Bring their words, their tone of voice and their habits of speech to mind.

2. Write their dialogue down.

Person 1 _____

Person 2 _____

Person 1 _____

Person 2 _____

Listen to Your Characters

Dialogue allows the reader to listen to your characters and experience them as individuals. Capture their voices on paper while they still resonate in your ears. In doing so:

➼ **make extensive use of favorite words and colloquial* sayings.**

"Dark as the inside of a pocket," my grandmother used to say.

"Two, two, two! Here me come," Max would call out when we played hide-and-seek.

➼ **use phonetic transcriptions*** (according to sound rather than grammar).

"Ain't no way, I sez ta dem, ain't *no way* yous guys gonna do this!" I can still hear my Uncle Jet telling us those amazing stories from his childhood in the city. It always seemed so exotic and remote to us—farm kids on the prairie.

◆◆ include the pauses or other mannerisms that characterized a person's speech.

"A man and a woman . . ." my grandfather would say, and then he'd fall silent and look down at his lap where his big plumber's hands were resting. He'd seem to be looking inside himself for the rest of his thought. It was useless to rush him or to change the conversation. He'd just interrupt in a minute to add on to what he'd been saying before. ". . . don't need to be afraid of arguing." he'd conclude. Meanwhile, I'd have drifted off into my own thoughts, and I'd wonder what he was talking about.

EXERCISE

1. Choose another photo that depicts two people.

2. For each recall the following as appropriate:
◆◆ favorite words or expressions
◆◆ accent or speech to be phonetically transcribed
◆◆ notable mannerisms

3. Use these notes to put together a dialogue:

Person 1 _____

Person 2 _____

Person 1 _____

Person 2 _____

Person 1 _____

Person 2 _____

How to Use Dialogue

You can use dialogue in your cameo narratives to record:

1. what people were saying to each other at the time of the photo or around that time.

"You coming to the corn roast tonight?" Jayne wanted to know. "Will there be dessert?" I asked. Of

63

all my cousins, she was the one I could tease the most. I still miss that banter and it's ten years now since she moved away. "If you get busy in this kitchen!" she shot back.

2. a typical conversation even if it was not spoken on the very occasion of a specific photo.

"What do you want to do?" my father used to ask me. "What sort of job do you think you'd be happy at?"

"I don't know," I'd answer.

"So what would you be good at?" he'd ask, trying again. And still I didn't know.

3. an individual's response to the photo many years later. A third person comment offers a glimpse into two characters, the speaker and her subject.

"Laura had many talents," her mother said to me at her daughter's funeral. "Did you ever hear her sing? Oh my! what a strong voice. I'd always have goose bumps when her voice filled the hall at Convocation!"

Using Foreign Words

Foreign words are fine—go ahead and use them. (You may need to check that you are preserving correct spellings!)

Of course, unless your family is still fluent in the language, it's awkward to use it extensively. But a few well-chosen words and phrases, especially when they are part of your memories, add interest without being difficult to understand. Words like *Mother, Father, I love you,* or the names of special foods or clothing in an original language are an affirmation of your family identity.

"Mon petit chou," my grandmother called us. No one's called me "my little cabbage" since!

Here are ways to make another language accessible in your album:

➥ include a translation in

64

parenthesis immediately after the non-English word—e.g. *placek* (a sweet Polish bread).

➺ paraphrase the word or phrase right away—*"Te amo,"* she said. "I love you." (This is the method that I generally prefer.)

Note that whenever you use a non-English word, it is *italicized* (or underlined if you are writing by hand).

Direct and Indirect Dialogue

While dialogue can make your writing come to life, not all dialogue is equally effective.

1. There are two kinds of dialogue: direct and indirect.

➺ **Direct dialogue is a straight quote.** The words a person spoke—or is alleged to have spoken—are used. Begin and end a direct quote with quotation marks. The tags *he said* and *she said* are placed outside of the quotation marks.

> "I made my best apple-blueberry pie ever just for you," said Mama.

Most of the time, it's best not to get fancy with dialogue tags. Using words like "she chortled" and "he riposted" can get out of hand quickly! Simplicity is best. It's the quote, after all, not the tag, that you want to make memorable.

➺ **Indirect dialogue is an allusion to speech.** It is introduced by "that." Indirect dialogue is an approximation—not necessarily the actual words. Indirect dialogue doesn't usually use quotation marks but sometimes does. (Quotation marks indicate that the speaker used those specific words.) Here are two ways to write indirect dialogue:

> Mama said that she had made her best apple-blueberry pie ever just for us.

> Mama said that she had made her "best apple-blueberry pie ever" just for us.

In the last example, the phrase "best apple–blueberry pie ever" is what Mama actually said; the rest is approximation. The quotation marks signal the reader that you have approximated what's not in them.

2. Direct dialogue makes a stronger statement than indirect dialogue. Test this by re-reading the examples above. The *direct* dialogue is more immediate; the *indirect* is less personal because the speaker is at one remove.

Although indirect dialogue has less impact, it is nonetheless an effective tool when you are uncomfortable or unable to attribute words directly:

> I remember Barb saying that we *shouldn't* bring it up to the group but Nancy insists that she said we *should* talk about it with the others.

Clearly this lacks the drama of:

> "Don't you ever raise that topic in the group," said Barb. "It's inappropriate and totally uncalled for!"

Tips for Writing Dialogue

1. You'll often need to approximate dialogue—whether direct or indirect. Is this okay? Well, it's inevitable. You didn't have a tape recorder to get the exact words. You are remembering what it was *likely* that your character spoke. So you approximate. Most dialogues in your album will be approximations. That's a good reason to keep it short. It's more likely to be authentic and less likely to be inaccurate that way. One day, you may be surprised to overhear another generation repeating your approximation as a "truth!" That's why it's so important to photoscribe your albums thoughtfully. Regardless of what really happened, your version of it, preserved in your album and read and re-read over the years, will become the "truth" as it is remembered from now on.

Children come up with some great phrases when they use new language skills to describe their discoveries in the world! Keep a notebook especially for writing them down right away.

2. Make your quotes sound like that person's voice. Ask that person if your quote is right, or, close your eyes and imagine them speaking to you. Listen with your "inner" ear. If you feel uncomfortable with what you write, take it as a sign that the voice is off.

3. Dialogue works best when limited to two to four exchanges. Often, a single exchange is enough. (One speaks, another answers.) You can also simply report what one person said without any response.

4. Dialogue can be included in several ways in a cameo narrative.

•➤ It can be most of the cameo narrative or all of it.

"Your aunt had music in her bones," Gran said. "That's her with the violin. Grandpa bought it from the music teacher. She took lessons for years. She'd always be asked to play when the family got together. And she started playing for weddings when she was just 15. Oh, she was *good*!" Her eyes would close, and I knew she was hearing her play and feeling her pride in her again.

•➤ **More than one dialogue can be placed in a single cameo narrative.** They should focus, however, on the same person, place, or thing (in this case, Uncle Nick's musical gift).

"Lee was my musical one," Gran said, "always 'playing music' on barrels in the barn or even on my pots and pans before Grandpa bought the fiddle."

"When she got to high school," my father once told me, Lee's music teacher told Gran and Grandpa, 'This girl has got to go to the Conservatory.' She got a lot of attention for that."

•• **Dialogue can be placed within a setting, a character portrait, or any other text.**

"Your aunt was a musical child," Gran said, looking at her gallery of family photos on the wall. They were all there, her parents, my grandfather, Mr. Al, her second husband, her children, (Mom and my aunts and uncles), my siblings, and all of her grandchildren. She pointed to a photo in the center.

Points to Remember

•• Dialogue is what people say. It adds variety and energy to your writing.

•• Dialogue expresses individual personality and character. It brings your characters to life.

•• Direct dialogue is a straight quote; indirect dialogue alludes to speech and isn't always in quotes.

•• Dialogue can stand alone or be part of a larger piece.

Chapter Seven

Using Action & Other Suggestions

By varying what you write in your cameo narratives you make your albums more interesting to read.

1. Using action–based cameo narratives will make your albums less static.

> The hill was long and well-iced. At night, the floodlights were on, but there deep shadows at the edge. The children ran hard from the wall to the crest of the hill and then jumped on the toboggan. They'd cling to each other, legs in the air. Someone would always fall off halfway down or they'd run into other sledders or hit the ski jump. Screaming, they'd tumble off in front of another sled, barely missing the stream at the bottom of the run.

•➤**The action you choose for a cameo narrative needn't be dramatic.** (Life's quiet moments make good cameo narratives, too.) Here's an example of quiet drama:

> Every day for ten years, I drove Route 9 to the high school. From several points on that road in the winter and early spring, I would see the White Mountains, especially the peak of Mount Washington, a hundred and twenty miles away.

•➤**Don't be reluctant to write about more momentous, life-changing events.** It is not in bad taste to write about tragic occurrences. Keep in mind to write simply and clearly, especially when dealing with difficult events.

> In this 1974 VW bus, Belinda and Jim took a trip to the west coast in 1978. The accident was only two years later. They were

coming home from a day in the city. There was freezing rain that night, and Jim must have hit a slick spot on the curve and lost control. The bus plunged down the cliff at Ocean Drive to those massive granite rocks where we used to climb as children. Belinda and Jim were dead. That was March 7, 1980.

Show your story, don't tell it. I can't overemphasize this! The reader must "see" your characters in actions that reveal their personalities and temperaments. Don't just *tell* how nurturing your father was. *Show* him *in the action* of nurturing someone.

Painting a vivid and colorful word picture is the secret to really effective and interesting photoscribing.

Imagine that, instead of writing, you are using a movie camera to tell your story. Movie cameras can only capture tangible details. They don't *tell* us that people are happy. They *show* us people being happy, doing happy things. With the movie camera model in mind, write the action itself. Don't write: *I was happy.* Write: *When Martin got the promotion, we kept catching each other suddenly smiling! All the tension of the last two years was gone.*

In the following narratives, note which **tells** that the mother was kind and which **shows** us how she was. Which cameo will your family will find more interesting and more convincing of your mother's kindness?

Cameo 1

Mother was always very kind to my high school friend, Tara, whose mother died when she was 14. One year she took her shopping for a winter coat.

Cameo 2

Mom noticed my friend Tara shivering as she waited for me before school. "Where's your winter coat?"

"It doesn't fit," Tara answered. "Dad's working overtime. I don't know when he can take me shopping."

"Well," said Mother looking at me pointedly. "Renée and I are going on Saturday. Why don't you come, too?" It was the first I'd heard that we were going shopping. That was my mother— she saw the need and just took care of it.

EXERCISE

1. Make a short list of people (2 or 3) in your life.

2. Brainstorm adjectives that describe each individual (e.g., beautiful, smart, kind).

3. Now, using the five senses, specifically show the meaning of the adjective. For instance, replace "kind" with a specific action (*put her arm around Amy and gave her a hug*) that *shows* her being kind.

4. Now write the stories which show the context of the adjectives you chose above. Include specific details (i.e., who was there, what was happening, etc.).

---

2. Include the best features of captions in your cameos. These are precise dates, full names of people and places, and references to relationships. Or, write both a caption with these details and a cameo narrative that is full of action, dialogue, setting, etc.

3. Avoid abstract words and phrases in your writing. This is a close cousin to **show, don't tell**. When words and phrases are vague, they conjure different images for different people. Although the reader always brings his own interpretation and experience to your writing, your specific words will guide his understanding as abstract ones cannot.

"We were poor when I was young," a friend once told me. The power of images to convey meaning was very clear to me when she added, "Our maid left every night after dinner. I was the only one of my friends not to have a live-in maid!" (That wasn't my definition of poor!)

71

Enable your reader to "see" everything you write—your characters, settings, and actions—by using specific and striking details. These are more likely to mean the same thing to different people. Writing in images will help you convey your meaning. Instead of writing *She was a pretty woman,* write what she looked like *(auburn hair, 5 foot 4 inches, fit and slender),* what she wore *(earth-colored corduroy jumpers)* and what her bearing was *(strode quickly).* Instead of *It was a big downtown,* describe the size of the stores, their color, shape, and construction *(square, three-storey wood–frame buildings).* What specific features of climate or vegetation were typical *(sugar maples* and not *trees)* and what were the winters like *(10 below* and not *cold, 18 inches of snow* and not *lots of snow).* Describe action with details, too.

On late winter days, I'd put on snow-shoes and pack Zoé on my back. I'd pull the toboggan full of sap buckets across the thinning snow as Zoé jumped up and down in the carrier, excited by the crisp air and the bright sun that cast lengthening shadows across the field. I'd ask over my shoulder as we went, "Zoé warm? Zoé like snow?" In the woods, I'd visit every maple in the grove. Zoé leaned over, pointing as I poured the cold sap into the big white buckets. Then, I'd feel her weight slump as she fell asleep against my shoulder. That was the beginning of several years of maple sapping with my children. It was a favorite time of year.

➺ **Be precise in your observations.** Don't use general phrases like *majestic mountain.* If the mountain is granite and has two peaks, write: *twin, granite-capped peaks.* If the mountain is completely forested with pines, write: *covered with pointed pines.*

4. Be sure to write about what is not pho-tographed as well as what is. A lifestory album is based on the Lifelist, not on the photos you happen to have on hand. Work with the story line of your Lifelist to become familiar with the gaps where life was lived but not photographed. These are perfect opportunities for cameo narratives.

E X E R C I S E

Free Writing

I. Write a cameo narrative for an event you for which you have no photograph.
➡ **Include facts** (names, actions, addresses), **feelings** ("I was so hopeful then"), **and impressions** ("warmest day," "proud of her hat"). Without giving any attention to style or grammar, write a journal-like entry for each topic or memory.

2. For each different memory, use a new page. Keeping one memory per page will help you to organize later. Concentrate on getting words on paper.

3. Use your free writing as source material. Having lots of notes is helpful when you combine or refine it later as you rewrite.

---

5. Include life's ordinary moments in your cameo narratives. Give yourself the assignment to write about a typical, not a special, day or activity. Where are the photos of you at work where you spend so much of your life or of you doing

My favorite moments of the day are early mornings when I'm the first one up having a cup of coffee on the deck.

mundane tasks such as laundry, dishes, driving, talking on the phone? Cameo narratives can capture memories worth preserving that may not make especiallly good photos. Instead of rushing to insert the camera between you and your experience, paint a word picture instead.

6. Lists—include parts of your Lifelist that you don't want to develop into stories of their own. In Chapter 2, I suggest that Lifelist notes should be brief—often no more than 3 to 5 words. You can include Lifelist items *as–is* in your album, or you may want to add text to make them meaningful. For instance, *barn cats* might become, *on the farm, there were always half-wild cats that never came in the house.* Think of the album page with your list on it. As you view the page, what will you need to say aloud to make the list meaningful? Writing that brief explanation in a complete sentence

Art Club Harvest Dinner

Menu: Mushroom rissoles, roasted vegetables, sage stuffing, *oignons doré,* pecan pie
Guests: Jane & Jay, Sylvia, John & Cole, Susie & Hank, Felice, Camie & Scott, Susan & Ron, Henri.
Decorations: waxed leaves and ribbons, berries with dried flowers, Jane'sshadow lights; gold, sienna, loden green linens.

ensures the story, however small, will be preserved and stand on its own.

List names of people, places, and favorite things. For example, to accompany a photo of you at thirteen, you might add a list titled, *My favorite songs in seventh grade.*

Recipes, menus, poems, prayers, songs, or sayings can also stand alone as cameo narratives, sharing more of the whole, moments of your complex life which your photos depict.

7. Maps, house and floor plans, drawings, tickets, programs—anything you want to include. Plan ahead to design all the elements: photos, text, artifacts and pages. Be sure to include cameo narratives to accompany artifacts as well as photographs.

8. Musings* make effective cameo narratives.
Musings *(I've always wondered. . .* or *What if . . .)* record your longings and reveal your imaginative life. Though a journal may be a more useful place for open-ended exploration of life choices, choosing to photoscribe important or characteristic musings adds a deeper level to your albums. This category may appeal more to older photoscribes who are looking back over a lifetime and evaluating decisions.and events.

EXERCISE

1. Write a Limited Lifelist that details your daily activities. If you have young children, you may be in that era when you can't believe you will ever be doing anything but changing diapers and picking up toys. But sooner than you think, your daily routines will be entirely different. Start today to do a Limited Lifelist of whatever occupies your days.

2. Use this list to generate both cameo narratives and photos of the ordinary moments you will cherish years from now. How about a word picture of doing the laundry?

3. Or, place your Limited Lifelist directly in your album or record your musings about that activity or time in your life.

Points to Remember

- Using action in your cameo narratives will add variety to your album.
- Show, don't tell. Let specific details convey your meaning. Abstract words and phrases mean different things to different people.
- Cameo narratives can vary greatly in their content.

Chapter Eight

Stage by Stage: A Writing Primer

Being aware of the different stages of writing—and their respective challenges and opportunities—will make you a more effective photoscribe.

The stages are **1) writing the rough draft,* 2) rewriting*** for more meaning and more precise meaning, and **3) editing*** the final copy. Each stage is important in creating a lifestory album and is creative and rewarding in its own way. In the exercises you have completed already, you have been directed in parts of each of these stages. In this chapter, you study them all together.

Stage One: the Rough Draft

The first stage of photoscribing is to write a rough draft on scrap paper. This is the raw material from which the final, polished cameo will be crafted.

I know that some people approach writing as a horrible, difficult task. Putting words down on paper is anxious and unpleasant for them. If you are new to the expressive writing of photoscribing or reluctant because of past lack of

I like being able to call it a "rough" draft—it frees me from having to be my perfect self all the time!

success, consider this: writing is like cooking!

You need a well–tested recipe (provided by this book), the raw ingredients (your life experiences and your photos assembled like so many vegetables and seasonings in a rough draft), and the willingness and time to do each step one after the other.

Write each rough draft on a separate piece of paper to make the later stage of rewriting easier.

But nobody's asking you to make a gourmet banquet for sixty! Begin to build your skills and your confidence with simple projects. If writing doesn't come easily to you, don't get discouraged. It **will** get easier.

There's no better way to learn to write than to write regularly. Just start putting down what comes to mind. Don't wait for just the right word or feeling. If you have something on paper, you can rewrite later, but you can't rewrite unless you've got something to work with!

Rough Draft Samples

Here are four rough drafts that tell four stories. I wrote the memories down just as they came to me while I lingered with this picture.

Cameo 1

My Ledoux grandparents always sat in different rooms, not like my other grandparents who were inseparable and always chatted with each other about anything and everything. I didn't think anything of this at the time. Now that I'm an adult I can see that perhaps they weren't well-matched. Maybe she was lonely in her marriage. She didn't get to show her playful side too much. He wanted order and regularity. I wonder if he was lonely, too.

Cameo 2

My grandmother Ledoux lived upstairs from us. She always played favorites. I happened to be one of her favorites. I know her choices were sometimes fickle. I think she felt that she and I shared similar interests and similar spirits. I appreciated something in her that Pépère and Dad and her other son, *mon oncle Léonard,* and Mom didn't.

Cameo 3

My grandmother Ledoux was, it seems to me, a woman who believed she couldn't have a good relationship to her sons but had to focus on her daughter. Unfortunately, her only daughter moved 3,000 miles away to California! Mémère was given to bouts of melancholia. Her relationship with Pépère—who was a silent and introverted man—didn't give her much relief. Two kids lived near her, but they were sons and I don't think she believed she could open herself to them.

Cameo 4

My grandmother Ledoux had a much lighter sense of herself and of life than Pépère did. He craved order and regularity; she craved disorder and spontaneity. They didn't resolve this difference over the years. There was always a tension between them about it. Although she's indulging her lighter side here and he is uncharacteristically submitting to it good-naturedly enough, this is not what I remember as typical.

In writing a rough draft, I let my imagination and my memory—rather than the photograph or my album—be my guide.

In the rough draft stage, don't worry about whether the writing is meaningful or polished. Your goal is to get words on paper. I set rough draft narratives aside in my *Photo Scribe Memory Binder* (see Soleil Press Directory, page 126) until I'm ready to work on them again. That comes after I've lingered with both photos and stories long enough to feel that I am telling the story I want to tell. Refering to my Lifelist helps me be sure not to omit an obvious link or another memory. Only when I'm confident my story is whole do I place the photos and final cameo permanently in my album. (See Chapter 9, "Putting It All Together.")

Don't be discouraged when you see the need for change. Most writing can be improved at every stage.

I have choices about how to use these cameos. They can be linked as one long piece. Or, I can keep them as short pieces interspersed throughout the pages that feature my grandparents. After all, each tells a different story about them and about my experience of them. Even if I use only one and discard the others, I have focused my memory on two important characters. Writing freely re-acquaints me with feelings and facts that inform my choice of what to include in the final draft. (See page 86, "Re-Writing Sample.")

Writing the rough draft is crucial in the overall process. The rough draft is always more than the sum of its parts. Writing uncritically at this early stage provides you with the most raw ingredients to work with.

EXERCISE

I. Choose several photos that are important to you. They should be picures you'd like to learn more about.

2. Write at least three cameo narrative rough drafts for each photograph. Write about a different aspect of the photo in each draft. Use dialogue, action, setting and character. Include sensory details to make your story come alive.

3. Review what you have written. What do you want to share and what do you want to keep private? Which of the rough drafts will you develop into finished cameo narratives?

Stage Two: Rewriting

Rewriting is the second stage of photoscribing. It's not a matter of just changing *these* words for *those*. It's a separate and essential stage of the writing process. Rewriting is your opportunity to communicate what you really mean.

Rewriting is finetuning. Ask yourself, "Is there anything I'm leaving out because I'm not yet aware of it, because I don't know *Some photoscribers find that rewriting is the most creative part of writing.* how to say it, or because I don't dare to say it?"

To answer these questions:

➨ **look inward.** Identify what you want and need to say.

➨ **review your Lifelist.** Linger with your photos to extract the most memory you can from them.

➨ **choose potent words and phrases.** These communicate the most meaning. Discard those worn–out flavorless words like *nice* and *good*.

This is the stage at which you make sure that you:

1. Double-check basic facts and relationships ascribed to your photos. Have you included the appropriate and accurate information: the *who, what, where, when, how,* and *why*? Are you sure—absolutely—about what you say you remember and the consequences of it? (We frequently make inferences from what we know. Unfortunately, we aren't always accurate.) Memories, as we've seen, can trick us: is it the event or the memory of it you are remembering? Perhaps

your cross-check or research will lead you to rewrite in order to give new information. Or you may decide to note that you are recording your version which hasn't been, or can't be, verified.

There are so many good ways to tell a story that you don't need to worry much about finding the one right way!

2. Focus each cameo narrative on only one character, action, or setting. Create a narrative that makes a focused statement:

> Jan spent that winter sorting out her things. She kept saying, "Simplify, simplify," as she carted box after box to Goodwill.

When you mix more than one focus in a single cameo, your writing loses its impact.

> Tony was a great gardener and he had a kayak.

The preceding example makes two statements. You can refocus the text around a single statement, or the second statement *(he had a kayak)* can go with another photo or as its own cameo. Here's a refocus:

> Tony always loved to be outdoors. He grew a large vegetable garden and took his kayak out on the river whenever he could.

By using an introductory sentence *(Tony always loved to be outdoors),* the parts of the cameo come together in one unified statement.

3. Blend character, action, setting, dialogue, and style in your cameo narratives. This full mix of writing elements adds variety and makes your cameo narratives more interesting and informative. This isn't a contradiction to #2 above where all elements are to be directed on creating one focus. These impart to your writing "soup" a rich-

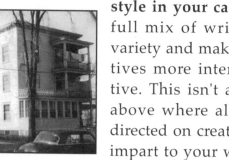

er flavor and entice your audience to read on. The following cameo is a rewrite of the short cameo above. Notice how much richer it has become thanks to the diversity of elements added during the rewriting stage.

> Tony was an outdoors type. I can see him now, hauling hay to mulch his garden, forking great clumps of soil to prepare the beds. "I'd love to spend some time with you," he'd say. "Why don't you come out to visit on Saturday?" And he'd grin hopefully, knowing I'd rather visit over cappuchino in town. "Coming out to visit" meant several hours of weeding and a death-defying kayak trip on the river as a treat.

4. Use the five senses in captions and cameo narratives to show rather than tell. Sensory details give your writing immediacy. Use specific sensations—taste, smell, sound, the color, texture, shape, and feel of objects—so your reader experiences them. Avoid the abstract *(a lovely smell)* in favor of the tangible *(the sharp scent of wet pine needles).*

In both short captions and cameo narratives, show rather than tell by use specific and striking details.

EXERCISE

1. Review at least five cameo narratives you have already written. (By now you have many on hand!)

2. Rewrite each following the guidelines mentioned above. Which points are the most difficult for you to adapt? Which are the easiest? Why?

3. Study differences between your rough drafts and rewrites. Do the rewrites have the best parts of the roughs?

The Rewriting Process

You can be more effective in rewriting your cameo narratives if you pay attention not only to *what* your text says but *how* it says it. Be willing to rework your writing. Why should it be perfect, first try?

1. Put your rough draft aside. Time—two days, a week, a month—will make you more objective and able to assess what your writing says and doesn't say.

2. Role-play reading your text with fresh, observant eyes and critical ears. Imagine you are a stranger who does not know you nor has any attachment to

your text. This person might say: "Let's see. Some cameo narratives by So-and-So. Are they any good?" Read from that imaginary person's perspective. Does your text seem interesting and meaningful? If not, make the necessary changes to correct the criticisms.

3. Show your writing to others for critique. Family feedback can be useful to add or corroborate information and details. On the other hand, friends who don't already know (and haven't lived through) your stories can alert you about where they lose the thread or don't "get it!"

When choosing a person to ask to help you in this process, be wary of the following:

➤ **People who make only supportive comments.** "Isn't that nice, dear, I like anything you do!"

Let other people organize their own lifestory albums if they have something different to say!

➤ **People who call *their* version of the story right and yours all wrong.**

You can, however, always learn something from feedback. A disagreement with a spouse or a relative may make you realize that the same story has more than one side and you should provide multiple versions for accuracy. In this case, write, *According to John, the kids at that age were . . ., but in my experience . . .*

Friends and colleagues will provide valuable perspectives different from your relatives' because they aren't under the influence of family rules and assumptions. They may tell you, "I don't understand why your sister did this. It seems out of character for the woman you describe in this other cameo narrative." Your reader might ask, "Why did your husband say that? It's not clear to me why you interpret it as supportive of you. He comes across as very cold."

We are all given (or trained) to take the pecularities of our own families for granted. New photoscribes can find they are simply repeating "hand-me-down" versions of a family's story. It's important work to discover the story "according to you."

4. Eliminate *clichés* and stereotypes. Check both captions and cameo narratives for *clichés (a spry 76 years young)*, stereotypes *(men don't know a thing about kids!)*, stale, cute phrases *(it's a girl thing!)*. Trade these *clichés* and stereotypes for phrases that convey real information based on specific and accurate details of setting, character, or action. (If these examples don't resonate for you, substitute an ethnic, religious or racial category you belong to so you get the point.) Stereotypes are not only weak writing, they separate us all from true understanding.

Replace trendy phrases, too, because they say little now and will mean even less in twenty years.

(Consider the once popular 1920's expression *twenty-three skidoo!*—now what *does* that mean?!)

Some people hoard words and phrases—they can't bear to throw any away!

5. Rework your text if you have to explain to make your point clear. Since you won't always be there to clarify, make your cameo narratives—either singly or in groups—so articulate that readers will understand immediately what you have said.

If you find you have to explain further, add what you say to your written text—or replace what you've written with what you're saying.

6. Find a friend and be a friend. Writing buddies can be very helpful as you write and re-write. Friends can not only tell you if your cameo narratives leave them wanting more or are unclear, they can also give

you encouragement. If it stimulates your creativity to share the design and production phases with fellow scrapbookers, you'll enjoy writing together, too. The companionship of a fellow photoscribe is rewarding and can be crucial to persevering at your work.

Re-Writing Sample

Remember the first drafts of cameo narratives I wrote for this photo on page 80? Here's my rewrite:

Walking in on my Ledoux grandparents in their upstairs apartment in the house we shared on the Ridge, I'd always find them sitting in different rooms. They wouldn't be chatting together like my other grandparents. While their silence didn't seem to bother Pépère, it did grate on my grandmother. Mémère was given to bouts of moodiness that her relationship with Pépère—a silent and introverted man—didn't help. As an adult, I wonder what it was about their relationship that didn't permit them to help each other more?

It's interesting to me that Pépère is so good--naturedly submiting to her teasing. He was usually more serious and he craved order and regularity. It's not a typical scene of them at all, not one that I remember. She must have been lonely. She didn't often show this playful, humorous side of herself.

Because I am a writer, my choice is usually to include more text rather than less in an album. You might choose differently. That's ok. Just make sure that your choices convey the maximum story you can tell, especially when you are recording family history for another generation.

Stage Three: Editing Techniques

Rewriting and editing are not entirely distinct activities. As you rewrite, you will also edit, and while you edit you will do some rewriting. But there is a key difference. As you re-write, you continue to produce text. **Rewriting is usually an expanding process.** As you edit, you are not usually adding more words. Instead, you are polishing the text that exists. **Editing is therefore often (but not always) a contracting process.**

Working on many cameo narratives at once can be an effective method.

There are certain points to keep in mind when you edit. Let's start with these:

1. Check spelling, grammar, and punctuation.

These aren't really monsters that enjoy making your life miserable. Think of them instead as tools that allow you to communicate effectively with your reader. By following conventions of spelling, grammar, and punctuation you make it easy for your reader to follow your lead.

2. Verify spellings for every name and foreign word you use. (This is so important that it deserves its own listing.) Think of Ellis Island—and the names that were changed forever. Your spellings may become documentation for the generations to come. Be sure you're not setting a false standard for them.

Remember: you're not just archiving photographs—you are recording a lifestory for posterity.

3. Examine your vocabulary to make sure that you have used words that your family can understand and identify with. Resist the urge to reach for a fancy turn of phrase. Better to write simple sentences and be proud of them than to sound foolish in an attempt to impress! *Simple* doesn't mean exhausted words like *nice* and *good*. Make every word carry its own weight of meaning.

4. Re–read for consistency. Consistency is a term which is broader than the term *focus* in its application. **Consistency means that each element in your narrative is in keeping with every other.** Your narrative, of course, needs to be focused on one character, action, or setting. It needs something more, however. Its vocabulary, type of sentence structure, point of view, and tone need to be consistent throughout the text. Consistency has to do with writing style and the mechanics of your prose.

5. Check for coherence. Your story must make

sense, and not wander off this way and that way. Coherence has to do with the ideas. They have to "hang together" and be clear as to what they mean. When someone says your writing is rambling, they most likely mean that it is not coherent. Clarity is a another word that is sometimes used to mean coherence.

6. Make your writing concise. Use as few words as you need to say just what you want to say. Eliminate redundancies, material that does not contribute directly to the overall impact of your captions or cameos. Being concise is always helped by the application of the ten percent rule: cross out one word in every ten in your text. Most writing can be improved by making it shorter and more to the point.

Points to Remember

- ➻ There are three stages to photoscribing: creating rough drafts, rewriting, and editing.
- ➻ The rough draft is the raw material of your writing.
- ➻ Rewriting is an opportunity to communicte what you really what to say.
- ➻ Editing is a stage of getting your language in line with convention.

Chapter Nine

Putting It All Together

The time has come to put your captions, cameos, photos, and artifacts together in your lifestory album. **The life you and your family have lived, and not the photos you have, are at the core of the story this album must tell.** Of course, the photos you have on hand form a visual focus, but what you see is never the whole nor the limit of your story.

In creating lifestory photo albums, you may find, as I have, that you have clusters of photos around a single event—one Christmas when the camera was new and the photographer was very enthusiastic. However, you may have no photo to document another time you remember well and which was perhaps even more significant—the winter when your father fell sick and died, for instance.

> Now it's all gone except for the memories...I've never forgotten those people—though with every passing year the voices grow dimmer.
> —Woody Allen, in "Radio Days"

That is why cameo narratives are so important. They tell the stories behind your photos, but they also tell the stories for which there are no photos. How you group these photos and narratives will be crucial.

Art gallery owners and museum directors will tell

you how important it is to hang a show well. That means arranging pieces in the best relationships to each other and to the white space around them on the wall. A properly-displayed show emphasizes the artist's vision while a poorly-displayed one obscures it.

The same is true for you albums: ones with well-grouped photos and cameo narratives will tell your story much more thoroughly and effectively than those in which photos and text are poorly arranged.

Many Photos

If you have many photos, you can be selective. Since the mid-sixties, we've taken multiple pictures of not just one event but of one pose or scene. The technology is so easy, we can produce more than we need.

Look at all these photos of the new car! I'd give anything to have a picture of Brian the last time he came.

You could photoscribe and scrapbook all your photos, but the cost in time and supplies may be prohibitive.

1. Select a smaller number of photos for your lifestory photo album:

➥ **Choose the best.** Look for subject, focus, print quality, composition (how subjects are positioned in relation to each other and the background).

➥ **Choose photos that tell a story beyond the immediate subject.** Look for plenty of details in the background. Don't automatically discard pictures that are not the best photographic quality. In two photos of family members at a reunion, for instance, one may give a clear background view of a piece of furniture you remember or of a favorite aunt. Use this background piece or person as a stimulus for a cameo narrative and tell a story you otherwise wouldn't.

➤ When you crop photos, don't throw out anything essential in the image. Pay attention to artifacts in the background that tell the story of your family or ethnic group. Decorations or objects familiar in your own childhood may be obscure but important clues when your children start exploring their heritage.

Cropping can be compared to the 1950's craze of cutting the elaborate headboards off Victorian beds to create a "modern" look. How wonderful it would be if our parents' and grandparents' had not modernized in this way and had left those old-fashioned beds intact! Don't give your kids reasons to say the same about unfortunate photo cropping!

➤ Favor photos that were generated by important moments rather than by random and artificial "photo-opportunities."

It's so easy to take photos today! We've all taken them of moments that are not (when all is said and done) particularly significant—or even interesting to us. These are not the shots of life's ordinary moments (you at the library checking a book out) which can provide a meaningful story for the future. What I'm calling "photo opportunities" are those poses that essentially connect neither to ordinary moments nor to meaningful ones. For instance, does a photo of Jason in a sombrero (which your husband Ray plopped on his head as you were leaving a Mexican restaurant at the mall) preserve any real information about your son or your family? Does it evoke a significant memory with associations and family history attached? Not unless you once lived in Mexico. . .

Acknowledge how much effort you invest in photoscribing meaningful albums by working with your most significant images.

2. Select the primary photos to include in your albums. Then take one or more of the following steps to preserve and make use of the extras:

•❖ **Label them clearly with a photo-safe pencil.**

•❖ **Write info on post 'em notes for temporary identification.**

•❖ **Store them in an archival envelope that marks the subject, time, and album where similar photos are to be found.**

•❖ **Trade them with relatives.**

•❖ **Keep them for your children.**

•❖ **Use them in a second album for a relative or friend.** A lifestory album makes a wonderful gift.

Few Photos

Before the mid-sixties, people took many fewer photos than they do now. A lifestory album requires that you not only tell the story behind your photos but that you tell the story of the missing photos, too.

1. When you have too few photos, cameo narratives can bridge the gaps in your story. Compare your Lifelist to the photos you have in your collection and other pictures you have access to. Wherever you have gaps, record the experience in a cameo narrative. These gaps may occur in any album but are more prevalent in a heritage album that seeks to tell lifestories from the past.

2. Artifacts can fill out or complete an album. These include photos, post cards, newspaper clippings that portray some phase of your life, or of the life of your subject.

In an album dedicated to your father who was a firefighter, why not include reproductions of historic photos of his fire station, tickets to the firemen's ball, an antique post card of the fire station, or a photocopy of an article from the local newspaper's archives—especially one in which he or his unit is mentioned.

For another page, you might include a recipe or the verses of a hymn, the map of a town or the floor plan of the house where you grew up. Include tickets and ribbons, etc. It's your album. Just put as much care into selecting and preserving your memorabilia as you do your photos. Use cameo narratives to make clear links between your artifacts, your photos, and the storyline they convey.

Heaven and earth shall pass away, but my words shall not pass away.
—Matthew 24:35

An institution that has played a role in the life of the person who is your subject is also a good focus for a multi–media album with photos, artifacts and cameos.

3. Today's photos of your life's important buildings and places can help you to document the past. Go to places that were important to you or to the person whose story you are telling. Photograph the house, for instance, where your parents lived when you were born. If you are aware of changes to the house, you can write, for instance, *the picture window in front was a later* *addition, replacing two small windows there.*

4. Photo editing technology now makes it possible to make new images from old. Not only can you repair damaged photos you can create new ones.

➔ **You can add or remove people and elements from photos.** For instance, you have no photos of your mother and her three sisters together. With computer programs now widely available, you can group them in a new composite image! (This is why photographs are no longer allowed as evidence in court.) You can

eliminate elements, too. Of course, when you alter images, you have a responsibility to let your audience know. To do otherwise is falsifying a record—and creating a lie. The explanation itself can be an important addition to your family story!

I removed my father's cousin from this photo. Mom and Dad borrowed money from him to buy their house on Ocean Street. He foreclosed on the loan when Dad was injured at work. Then he turned around and sold the house for a big profit. I couldn't bring myself to include him in this album.

➔ **You can improve elements in your pictures.** Change colors, eliminate obtrusive backgrounds, lighten dark areas, bring a face out of the shadows. You can eliminate stains and creases and proportions.

Print your altered photos (or get them printed) on photo–safe paper on a high resolution printer. All these services are available in home computer software or by working with a professional. Look in the Yellow Pages under *Photo Retouching and Restoration* for specialists near you.

Organizing Your Photo Albums

1. Use the following suggestions as organizing principles for placing your cameo narratives and photos in an album:

⟶ Chronology

Most photoscribes choose to organize their albums by time. Arrange your photos and texts in the same sequence as the events they portray or describe. Childhood, youth, middle-age, then retirement; spring, summer, fall, then winter. Chronology always offers a natural progression for an album.

⟶ Theme

You may want to organize some or all of your albums around specific topics or events. A theme album can feature photos and cameo narratives that celebrate career, marriage, vacations, or a new home. A theme album's internal organization is often chronological.

⟶ Character (Biography)

You can focus your album on one person's life. Such commemorative albums are especially cherished at times of celebrations or of loss. Mother's Day, Father's Day, graduation, the death of an individual. When biography is your main focus, you also have the choice to develop your albums with an internal organization by chronology (birth to present day) or theme (career, for instance).

⟶ All of the above.

Although you may begin to photoscribe your lifestory albums by one of these, you will likely find yourself combining all of them. There is no one correct way. You may want to interrupt the chronological order of several albums to create a theme album for the birth of a child, the story of a house being built, or a special celebration.

2. The Lifelist remains the inner core of your albums' organization. However you conceive of your photo albums always refer to your Lifelist for cues about how to organize your albums.

Placing Narratives in Your Albums

Where do you place your cameo narratives in the pages of your photo albums? Here are some suggestions:

1. When you have more photos than cameo narratives, place cameos on the page as you do photos. Using the layouts you have perfected, create attractive pages in which both the photos and the text serve as design blocks.

Both the text and the photos will be enhanced by color backgrounds, borders or other design elements such as cut–outs or decals. Your choice of period-appropriate colors and headline fonts can enhance the stories you are telling.

Don't let your page design overpower readability.

2. When you have more cameo narratives than photos, however, you may find that your album doesn't look "right." You may feel you have too much text. Use the following ideas to integrate the narratives into your pages:

Creating text-only or text-predominant pages doesn't mean you have to give up on unique page layout designs.

➼**Write or print the many cameo**

narratives on photo-safe paper—no other kind is appropriate for your albums. Insert text pages between photo pages. You can label photos and corresponding cameo narratives with the same number to match the two. Interleaving text pages between photo pages is effective if you write long stories, too.

Whether you choose to write by hand or by computer, you can vary the style of your layout and size of lettering. Writing or printing, you can vary the length of lines and the shapes of text blocks from page to page, or from album to album.

Of all that is written, I love only what a person has written with his blood.
—Nietsche

Your album is a book, after all. As you design, be sure to look critically at books and magazines that come your way. What elements please you? The symmetry and balance that visual uniformity creates over the span of one album or a series of albums will allow the storyline to dominate.

Well-placed variations add flavor—titles askew or blocks at an angle draw attention. If you make variety the rule, however, watch out for the busyness and the clutter of too many jazzy designs. Too many styles and shapes on one page can detract from the story.

•• **Write directly on or affix text pages to your album pages.** Whetehr you write by hand or by computer, you can create text pages with empty blocks for photos. The photos accompany and illustrate the text around them.

•• **Design a marginal column for the photos or the text. Separate the two sets one off from the other.**

•• **Use expandable albums into which you can insert additional pages anywhere—whether photos**

or text. When you use an expandable album, you can insert narrative pages (either of a uniform size or the same size as the photo pages) between the photo pages. Be sure to label each photo (with a number system for instance), and each cameo narrative correspondingly. Interleaving with parchment or tissue (like wedding invitations) between written and photo pages will protect the photographs from scuffing.

Points to Remember

- ❧ When you have many photos, choose those that tell the most of your story as well as have the best photographic quality.
- ❧ When you have few photos, supplement them with cameo narratives to carry the storyline.
- ❧ When you place photos and cameos together in your albums, choose design elelments that favor both.

Appendices

Appendix A

The Whole Story—Even If It's the Truth?

It may seem a simple matter: of course, you'll tell the truth! But it's inevitable that sooner or later you'll encounter a decision about **what** to tell and **how** to tell it—and there'll be no simple answer in sight!

Do you really want to write, for example, that the smiling woman in the background was your father's mistress? How do you say that your cousin who left town quickly was not really an embezzler—do you write that he was merely a sloppy bookkeeper?

When you speak to relatives about your common ancestors or when you check documents and records, do you learn that the story you've always believed to be true is not at all? You may conclude that someone has lied or not been entirely frank. In choosing what version to preserve follow your heart and keep these guidelines in mind.

1. Your unhappy memories need to be verified, too. Ironically, we can be attached to our angry or sad memories and not want to verify them—for fear of having them disproved. Could the unsettling memory really be about you or a certain time in your life rather than about another person? A person or

Write the story your intuition tells you is true. Or you can choose not tell the story at all.

experience in an unhappy moment in your life may be tainted with the misery of that time.

Just as you can verify air temperature by reading a thermometer so too, you can verify life facts—even the sadness—by consulting the right gauges: relatives, documents (letters, diaries, newspaper accounts, certificates, diplomas), and public records (birth, census, death, tax, among others).

•• **Your own version of the truth may depend on your point of view.** Point of view refers to the "eyes" of the narrator from which the story is seen or understood. Your point of view always limits and colors what you know and consider to be true. But you may decide that there are other ways of looking at things besides yours—all or none of which may reflect what really happened or what you want to believe happened.

How Much is Too Much?

When you want—or feel you should—tell the truth, how much is too much—both for you and for your viewers? Keep the following in mind:

1. Concealing information can significantly alter a reader's interpretation of the life, theme, and events your lifestory album portrays. You risk lying to your family when you knowingly keep the truth hidden from them.

An instance of this, in one of the famous published diaries of the twentieth century, is Anaïs Nin's celebration the freedoms of her life as an artist. She did not tell, however, that she was not living off income from her writing but was being bankrolled by a husband—a fact she never mentions, not even once! Her *Diary* might have spared many young writers the pain (and disappointment) of modeling their lives on hers!

In withholding an important piece of information as you recreate family history, might you be doing a disservice to your family as Nin did to young artists?

2. Photoscribing is not the opportunity to attack or expose anyone! Being the author doesn't give you permission to conscript someone for your side of an argument. When someone tries to engage you on his side, don't you feel that your good will is being taken advantage of? Your family will feel the same as they read your  vengeful (or tell all) cameos—especially in an album you have given them as a gift!

Exposing someone when no good can come from it is also a questionable photoscribing practice. Next to a picture of your sister, you just don't need to write:

> Here's Annie before her secret marriage. What a mess that was! She and her husband ran up credit cards like crazy . . .

If you know it will hurt someone close to you to give out certain information in your album, why divulge it? (Isn't it time to examine the tangle of feelings that makes you want to go ahead with such behavior?)

3. You don't have to write anything you don't feel comfortable telling. You have the right to privacy. Your albums don't have to reveal details that you don't want to share.

Maintaining relationships and your dignity as a person may be more productive than telling all. Your albums, one can safely state, are not the place to confront uncomfortable or compromising truths. Setting appropriate boundaries is not only perfectly okay, it is also desireable and necessary.

Points to Remember

- ⮞ Telling the truth is not a simple matter.
- ⮞ Unhappy memories need to be checked.
- ⮞ Don't use your photoscribing as an opportunity to attack someone.
- ⮞ You always have a right to remain silent.

Appendix B

Unsettling Memories

Recording your lifestory by photoscribing your albums will stimulate your imagination to re-enter a world that no longer exists—the world of your past. Sometimes this experience brings pleasure and you welcome the memories. At other

They're all gone now. It's hard doing a lifestory album.

times, however, the memories are disturbing and unwelcome. Perhaps it is not a specific memory that surfaces as you look at your photos, but a faint sadness, a vague unease.

Not Only Happy Moments

Photographs are generally taken of happy moments, occasions of family and personal celebrations when smiles are on every face.

As you spread out pictures, perhaps for the first time in years, you may relive scenes with parents and siblings, children, spouse, friends, or partners. You re-visit the world portrayed in your photos. Suddenly, unannounced, unwelcome, comes a memory you had forgotten or kept at bay. Perhaps it's of poverty, or abuse, abandonment, failure, or addiction, illness or loss. Or, you begin to think of missed opportuni-

It's odd—I thought all my childhood memories were bad ones. But as I wrote cameos about my parents, I realized they just did the best they could. They weren't really cut out to be parents. I guess you could say I forgive them.

ties and decisions not made, of relationships allowed to go bad. Something in a photo—or, what it reminds you of—jumps out at you. Perhaps as you linger with a photo taken on your tenth birthday party, you see there the neighbor or family friend or place that played a role in a painful dispute or loss. The memory ambushes you after all this time.

I am a survivor. I've worked hard to limit the ripple effect of my long, unhappy childhood.

➦**The part of you still hurt by this memory is the child, not the adult, self.** Your child-self, by its very nature, feels abandoned, neglected, and undervalued. (We all carry with us this resident child and can be dominated by it no matter what our age.) Your adult-self, on the other hand, is always capable of protecting, nurturing, and helping. (That part of ourselves is with us, too, whatever our age—even as children.)

Only you can assess your comfort level.

➦**You can choose to keep your child-part in perspective and your adult-part in control.** Let your adult speak reassuringly to your child-self: "I know reliving this is difficult. I am here and I will keep you safe. You don't have to be with this person or in this circumstance ever again." Or, "This is painful but you are safe here in the present."

➦**Make the positive choice not to let negative feelings and thoughts dominate you.** If you let them float away they will diminish in time. Coming across the photo of an individual who wronged you may fill you with helpless anger. But you are not helpless now. You can choose a strategy that ensures you are not overtaken once again: let those negative thoughts go (no matter how justified). Practicing this habit works.

An Effective Tool

Writing is an effective and powerful tool for working through difficult memories. Creating lifestory albums may help you to come to terms with sadness and discomfort. While the experience of photoscribing painful memories isn't pleasant, it has benefits:

I'm not that way now. It's unpleasant to go back and see the person I was then.

➨**understanding what happened.** For some people, knowledge can lead to release.

➨**diminishing negative feelings.** When memories are worked with in a non-judgmental way, they lose their intense charge of feeling. Holding on can keep them burning.

➨**lessening of anger.** Sometimes it is helpful to vent sorrow or pain on paper (but not necessarily to share that writing). After such a catharsis, we feel better.

The process of dealing with unsettling memories is more significant than producing finished albums. Deal honestly with painful life-facts first. Then decide whether to share or not.

Accepting a painful or sad experience can transform you from a victim into a person who is ready to move on. In this healing, your writing is a confidant, an ideal listener.

The Indirect Approach

You can best approach some pain indirectly. For instance, if the death of a loved one is still too raw, try organizing photos about other people, events, or eras s/he was not central to. Eventually, like peeling an onion, layer by layer, you will begin to approach the

Photoscribing is not a substitute for counseling, if you are dealing with trauma. But in many instances, it has therapeutic benefits. center of your grief—and move towards acceptance and understanding. As you do so, you can write about this person with greater ease and allow yourself to re-experience more positive memories of them, too.

When you feel ready, begin to work with the photos you associate with pain or discomfort in your past and give preserving your difficult stories a try.

Points to Remember

- •◆ Making a lifestory album is sure to bring up some unsettling memories for most of us.
- •◆ Photoscribing is an effective tool for dealing with emotional pain. It is not, however, a substitute for counseling or therapy.
- •◆ Dealing with pain indirectly is a viable choice.

Appendix C

Sample Cameo Narratives

In the following examples I have written for a bio-graphical heritage album about my father, I use long cameo narratives to fill in the gaps between photos. Even if I had more photos, they couldn't tell the whole story that needs to be told in these cameos. Only the addition of cameo narratives and informative captions can fill the gap between photographs and life as it is lived.

These two cameo narratives depend on dialogue for their development. The first is a transcript of two conversations. It appears on a page which features photos of my father and me. In one of these, for instance, he is holding me, age 10 months, on his knee, in the fall of 1947. He's wearing an overcoat and I am all bundled up in a hooded one-piece suit:

"Why didn't Dad do the GI Bill?" Mom said to me in 1998. "He was a smart man. He could have gotten a good job for himself if he'd gotten a degree then. A lot of fellows did that when they got out of the service after the war. It just didn't interest him that much, I guess."

I remember my mémère saying to me when I was an adolescent, "We had the money to help him then. He could have stayed in school. He didn't want to."

This cameo narrative reveals something about my father that is not seen in the photo of the young man holding his baby son on his lap. Yet it is important information. At the time of this picture, undetected by the camera, his decision not to pursue an education was one that would have serious consequences for him and his family. The cameo narrative explains him and, with others, creates a portrait that would otherwise be lost. It's part of his—and consequently my— larger story and I want to preserve it in my album.

The second cameo narrative is not about the character of an individual but a community. It is a remembered version of a conversation in which my father himself "speaks" here. I transcribed this conversation from memory many years after it was spoken.

> "When I was little, we lived down on Bates Street [the tenement district]," my father told me. "Children didn't misbehave. They knew they couldn't without everyone knowing. If a kid was naughty, a mother in a nearby apartment would throw a window open and stick her head out, 'Go home right now. What do you think you're doing? You know better than that! I'll see your mother tonight at the Ladies of St. Anne! She's going to be mad when she hears about this!'"

The photos I have of my father include those of his First Communion and of his confirmation, but I have none of him in daily activity in the district where he grew up. I include the previous cameo narrative

among the photos of celebratory moments because I want to tell the full story of what his childhood was like. The woman who flung open the window didn't doubt for a moment that other mothers would welcome her intervention. She expected the same from them.

Photoscribing allows his grandchildren and their (future) children to learn that communities in their

Pépère's day were cohesive and not at all anonymous.

Here are two more cameo narratives that fill a story gap in my photo album. They come from a Lifelist I did for my father's life. They feature setting. In them, I describe in two separate ways the neighborhood to which my father moved as an adolescent. It was uptown in an area of single homes with little yards.

> The Farwell Street neighborhood reflected a change as mill workers moved out of downtown to outlying districts. In 1936, these areas of town were developing fast. Holy Family parish had been organized in 1923 but it was still celebrating its liturgy out of a basement church on Sabattus Street.
>
> For my grandmother Ledoux, Holy Family was always a temporary parish, not a fit replacement in her heart for the huge, gothic Sts. Peter and Paul whose spires dominated the downtown skyline after its completion in 1938. She had contributed regularly to its construction and had followed the liturgy there since 1916.

This cameo narrative tells you something about both the neighborhood at that time and my grandmother. The next one focuses on my father's neighborhood more specifically.

> The Farwell Street neighborhood may have been far from the city's cramped downtown but it was still full of family.
>
> Highland Avenue was perpendicular to Farwell Street. Dad's aunt (his mother's sister) Rosilia and her husband, Thomas Beaulieu, lived there in a house almost identical to the Ledouxs'. They had two sons, René and Roland, who were Dad's age. Then, two houses away was another, older cousin, Rosa Labourdais (her mother was Dad's aunt and godmother, Ernestine Bilodeau Rioux). Rosa lived there with her husband and children. Four houses beyond lived another cousin, Albert Lizotte, (his mother was Dad's aunt Angéline Bilodeau Lizotte) with his wife Aline and daughter Fernande.

Later, when Dad married the girl next door, he added to his neighborhood a set of parents-in-law and an uncle and aunt-in-law (Albin and Augustine Lessard).

These cameo narratives are on a page with photos of the Ledouxs on their lawn at 49 Farwell St. They are the only photos I have of this period so I use narrative text to reveal key elements of the setting that a photo of smiling relatives in the yard can't.

This example, by contrast, features an action to convey its portrait.

This photo was taken c 1960 Pépère was a foreman at the Bates for 42 years.

In the mornings (before he moved out to Farwell Street in 1936), William walked from his apartment to the Bates Mill with the thousands of other operatives who descended from their tenements—in the cold dark of winter, in the cool light of summer—to fill the street. People came for the seven o'clock shift from New Auburn across the river, from the narrow, twisted streets of Little Canada, and from the neighborhood north of the park where the apartments were larger, more modern and expensive. Workers filled the streets, on their way to the Bates, the Hill, the Androscoggin, the Pepperell along the Canal and the Continental, by the powerful Androscoggin River.

In the afternoon, at 2:45, the workers flooded the streets again as men and women came for the second shift—the latecomers rubbing shoulders with the first shift who trudged home for an early supper and rest.

Each example features one aspect but includes others too: the above narrative is based on an action, but is strong on setting. The following is also an action-based narrative with a strong emphasis on setting.

In those days before road salting and modern plows, Bartlett Hill was closed for the winter. The tenement children gathered on cold, bright afternoons to slide. Bartlett was a clear, steep hill that started where Androscoggin Avenue is today. From there you can see the towers of City Hall and St. Patrick's Church (but not yet Sts. Peter and Paul which was completed only in 1938). As my father grew up, the construction continued and the church with its gothic spires rose over the city— every year a more spectacular cityscape  to see from Bartlett Hill. Their sled ride ended at Mailhot's Sausage at the bottom, a long exhilirating run that would be the subject of many animated conversations the next day at the school recess at St. Peter's School.

Resources Appendix

Glossary of Terms

action: see plot.

annotate: to complement with short, explanatory written material. Photoscribes use captions to do this.

autobiography: an account of the writer's own life; often used interchangeably with the terms *memoir* and *lifestory*.

caption (photo caption): information labels placed near photos as brief phrases or bulleted lists; also called annotations.

background: the part of a photo situated behind the subject(s) which are depicted, as opposed to *foreground*.

biography: the written account of the life of another person; often used interchangeably with *memoir* and *lifestory*.

cameo narratives: short lifestory narratives, generally 50 to 150 words—although they can be shorter or longer.

cast of characters: the "actors" or people who are central to the photo caption, cameo narrative, and/or lifestory photo album.

cliché: a trite, stereotyped expression that has lost originality and impact by long overuse. It usually contains a kernel of truth.

colloquial: characteristic of familiar or everyday conversation rather than of formal speech or writing.

dialogue: a conversation between two or more persons.

edit: to correct for grammar and spelling and to check for consistency, coherence, completeness, and conciseness.

Extended Lifelist: a Lifelist which contains the memories of an entire lifetime.

foreground: the front and often the focus or subject of the photo, as opposed to *background;* most often what we want to preserve.

Lifelist: a list of any and all memories of people, events, feelings, longings, etc. Includes both the Extended and the Limited Lifelist.

lifestory: a story of a life, usually created in independent segments which do not need to be linked with one another as in an autobiography. The term is often used interchangeably with *autobiography,*

biography, and *memoir.*

lifestory photo album: a photo album, composed of narrative text and photos, which tells an autobiography or a biography.

Limited Lifelist: a Lifelist which contains the memories of a specific event, theme, or era.

memoir: a part of an autobiography dealing specifically with presenting a comprehensive view of a time or activity; often used interchangeably with autobiography, biography, and lifestory.

musings: ruminations or "what if" thoughts that reveal the writer's internal or imaginative life.

narrative: an account of events and experiences told in prose. In a lifestory album, narrative is told in photographs, in words, and/or in a combination of both.

phonetic transcription: dialogue which records conversation or speech according to pronunciation rather than correct or standard spelling and grammar.

photo caption: see caption.

photo-safe: acid-free and lignin-free as well as ph neutral and stable; high quality materials that will not destroy your narratives and photos over time are photo-safe.

photoscribing: the process of writing expressive texts and combining them with photographs in order to create a lifestory photo album.

plot (action): the action of the story.

rewrite: to fine tune, improve and re-work texts for clarity, feeling and description. To rewrite is to revise.

rough draft: the first, raw text which will be rewritten and edited.

setting: the surroundings and environment as well as the culture and time period in which the story of your text takes place.

storyline: A synonym for narrative.

vignette: a short, meaningful narrative, a self-contained mini-story.

voice: the authentic quality and character of a particular personality; in writing, authenticity of representation.

Bibliography

I have found the following books helpful to myself and to my writing students. This is not a comprehensive list.

Albert, Susan Wittig. Writing from Life / Telling Your Soul's Story, Jeremy Tharcher/Putnam, NY, NY. 1996. *Though focused on women's lives, Wittig's writing models offer good advice for all lifewriters. More process– than finished product–oriented.*

Hagberg, Janet O. Wrestling with Your Angels / A Spiritual Journey to Great Writing, Adams Publishing, Holbrook, MA. 1995. *Excercises to deepen awareness and discipline through the craft of writing.*

Kempthorne, Charlie. For All Time / A Complete Guide to Writing Your Family History, Boynton/Cook/Heinemann, Portsmouth, NH. 1996. *Covers much of the same ground as Turning Memories Into Memoirs. A good read. Accessible.*

Kowit, Steve. In the Palm of Your Hand / The Poet's Portable Workshop, Tilbury House, Gardiner, ME. 1995. *A lively guide for the practicing poet and for those interested in perfecting style.*

Maisel, Eric. Fearless Creating / A Step-by-Step Guide to Starting and Completing Your Work of Art, Jeremy Tharcher/Putnam, NY, NY. 1995. *This book is masterful in making clear and accessible each step of the creative process.*

Scrapbook Guild. The Simple Art of Scrapbooking, The Scrapbook Guild/Dell Paperback, NY, NY. 1998. *An excellent book for creative treatment of scrapbook form and content. Not a writing book, not a page layout book; of special interest to photoscribes.*

Selling, Bernard. Writing from Within / A Guide to Creativity and Life Story Writing, Hunter House, Alameda. CA. 1998. *The subtitle says it all. Especially for those who want writing to lead them deeper. Solid writing suggestions for all levels.*

Albums & Other Supplies

Creati Memories

Creative Memories provides photosafe supplies and album—making instruction through its consultants' workshops and classes.
Creative Memories
2815 Clearwater Road
St. Cloud, MN 56302-1839
800-468-9335

Mail Order Sources: A Partial List

20th Century Products (see web listing)
PO Box 2393
Brea, CA 92822
800-767-0777

Aiko's Art Materials
3347 North Clark Street
Chicago, IL 60657
773-404-5600

Kodak
343 State Street
Rochester, NY 14650
315-253-1486

Scrapbook Company Catalog
1115 North 200 East, Suite 140
Logan, UT 84341
888-750-6844

Scrappin' & Stampin'
33221 Plymouth
Livonia, MI 48150
313-266-3014

Web Resources

This list is just to get you going on the web— every site will offer you links to others of interest!

www.amazon.com
This well-known on-line bookstore catalogues over a million books, including writing, craft and scrapbooking titles.

www.personalhistorians.org.
This is the site of the Association of Personal Historians whose members are professionals teachers or service providers in memory preservation via writing, audio— and videotaping.

www.creatingkeepsakes.com
This is the site of the popular idea-filled scrapbooking magazine. It includes current issues, newsletter, online store, a scrapbooking retail store locator, subscription info and friends forum.

www.familychronicle. com
Family Chronicle is a genealogical magazine. The website includes current and back issues, links to genealogy sites, subscription information, a surname origin list and tips for beginning genealogists.

www.geocities.com/Heartland/2878
The Family Photo Historian website includes many links to other genealogy and scrapbook sites, preservation classes, book and magazine reviews, free product catalogues, family charts.

www.gracefulbee.com
This site offers a myriad of products and a zillion links to other sites of interest.

www.memories.com
Memories is a scrapbooking supply company with over 6000 products. Their website includes an online catalog, scrapbook tips, and a retail store locator.

www.memorymakers.com
Memory Makers is a popular and beautifully designed scrapbooking magazine. The site includes current and back issues, archives of page ideas, and subscription info. Submit your own page layouts online.

www.tapestryintime.com
At the Tapestry in Time website, you can purchase products, peruse layout ideas, and share yours online.

www.20thcentury.com
20th century is a photo and album supply catalog selling 3-ring binder style albums, photo sleeves, and other photo storage products in both photo-safe and vinyl.

Index

Soleil Press Directory
Resources for Photoscribes, Lifewriters, and Teachers

Soleil Press

Soleil Press is a publishing company dedicated to producing high quality instructional materials and seminars for people who preserve their personal and family stories through written memoirs and lifestory photograph albums.

Founded in 1988 by author and teacher Denis Ledoux, whose autobiographical fiction was the company's first publication, Soleil Press is now the publishing arm of the international Turning Memories Into Memoirs Network of Lifewriting Teachers.

Publications

Photoscribing

The Photo Scribe, A Writing Guide: How to Write the Stories Behind your Photographs 16.95

The Photoscribe's Memory Binder 21.95
(custom 3-ring binder to organize your photoscribing projects)

Photoscribe Worksheets *for your classes (100 per tear-off pad):*
Writing Great Cameo Narratives 9.95
Writing Great Memory Lists 9.95

Lifewriting

**Turning Memories Into Memoirs
A Handbook for Writing Lifestories** 19.95

The Lifewriter's Memory Binder 21.95
(custom 3-ring binder to organize your lifewriting projects)

The Turning Memories Audio Guide 16.95
excerpts from the Handbook in a 120-minute, two-tape set)

Genealogy

The Genealogist's Memory Binder 21.95
(organize your genealogy & your ancestor's lifestories)

Ordering Information

Please call for shipping and handling charges. Orders accepted by phone, e-mail, or post; Visa and Mastercard, personal checks, purchase & money orders. Soleil Press memoir/photoscribe product lines are growing! Please request updated info on new materials and products to support your photoscribing, lifewriting, and family history projects!

Become a Lifewriting Teacher!

If you have a writing and/or teaching background, becoming an Affiliated Lifewriting Teacher could be the exciting next step in your professional development. As a Soleil Press Affiliate, you can earn either full- or a part-time income doing creative work that's truly significant— for you and for your community.

The Network of Lifewriting Teachers is an international affiliation of writing professionals in four English-speaking countries and throughout the US. They are committed to and experienced in assisting people to write their personal and family stories through workshops, seminars, and programs using the Turning Memories™ and Photo Scribe methods, materials, and curricula.

We invite you to contact us for more information about how our comprehensive and well-proven materials can launch or revitalize your workshop career. Call 1–888–80–STORY today.

Materials For Workshop Leaders

Presenter's Full & Partial Support Packages

(Please inquire for details: packages include Web Page ad, Consultation, and network support materials: Handbook, Audio Guide, Memory Binder, Curriculum (multiple models & syllabus) and Presenter's (a comprehensive course in effective workshop presentation) Manuals, Publicity Template Disk, Quarterly Newsletter, volume discounts on participant materials.)

1 –- 888 – 80 – STORY
(1-888-807-8679 ✳ 9 AM - 5 PM, EST, please
Visit our World Wide Web Site:
www.Turningmemories.com

Sponsor a workshop in your town!

Denis Ledoux conducts memoir writing and photoscribing workshops and presents programs at conferences and conventions. Is your organization, club, or unit looking for a dynamic speaker or workshop leader on a meaningful topic? Contact the office for details and booking information. Ask about Affiliate workshops near you, too.

When I was five we lived in the house on the hill. It was a magical place: an old New England farmhouse surrounded by a nine acre wood and high grassy meadow overlooking the river and the town. On the river side, the land tumbled away down a cliff--a craggy granite ledge which a former owner had equipped with a Victorian iron railing and a crudely cut path and steps. I would imagine I was one of the ladies, with a parasol in my grandmother's photographs as I tripped along the path in delicately heeled high-button shoes, carrying the train of my traveling costume. It was our favorite way to reach the road below and provided wonderful sites for hide-and-seek! Deep in the wood was a mica mine- treasure in the heart of darkness! Standing behind the house a row of tall pines- giant pines to a five-year-old -! a broad swing with ropes reached up into the sky...the smell of pine needles and the sense of height, the soaring whoosh! of pine boughs, and the dizzy motion of ecstatic swinging all come back to me when I remember the house on the hill. We lived there only one year while the church found a parsonage on a more sedate and prestigious street. But for me, the house on the hill with its atmosphere of links to the past and to nature, its elevation above the town and in my mind above the river will always be the seat of childhood fantasy, filled with the sounds and color and scents of imagination, the dreams of darkness and adventure that continue to feed my soul as an adult. and an